T0065371

THERE IS NO
LOWER HUMAN LIFE FORM
THAN AN IMMATURE 7TH GRADE BOY

RUSSELL C. MORROW

authorHOUSE

AuthorHouse™
1663 Liberty Drive
Bloomington, IN 47403
www.authorhouse.com
Phone: 833-262-8899

Published by AuthorHouse 11/09/2020

ISBN: 978-1-6655-0641-0 (sc)
ISBN: 978-1-6655-0640-3 (e)

Library of Congress Control Number: 2020921616

Print information available on the last page.

Contents

Foreword

While others may lead compartmentalized lives, Russell does not. He remembers exactly what it was like to be a 7th grade boy seeking acceptance and blurring the lines of obedience. Russell has taken and used those experiences with him, whether in his role as a teacher, Counselor, Vice-Principal in charge of discipline, or Principal.

I had the pleasure of working with Russell in an alternate universe, called middle school. Russell listened to each child as if he or she was the only child. He empowered them simply be giving them his full attention. He was passionate and compassionate about their circumstances, whether they were bereft at not making first string on a sports team or they were being abused or neglected at home. I heard Russell say to many kids, "You might not have much control of the circumstances at home, but here you can define yourself." He changed lives!

Russell has been a good friend for many years and his loyalty is a very important part of his humanity. He is able to see the irony and humor in his own behavior, both past and present, while understanding the vulnerability in others. He is able to reassure and inspire those with whom he works.

In this book, he exposes his own childhood behavior and brings it full circle to the students he mentored. You will undoubtedly recognize yourself in some of these portraits. You will smile, nod your head knowingly, and may even recall someone from your young life who, like Russell, saw similar juvenile behavior in you and reached out to help. Russell Morrow is a great guy with a unique insight that you will enjoy.

Former Co-Worker

After being formed and shaped from mud and water, through gentle human strength and imagination, jars of clay are tempered by fire and time. Some become brittle and break and some are strong enough to last through millennia, such as those that held the Dead Sea Scrolls.

Reading Russell's experiences as a student, young man, and educator brought this analogy immediately to mind. His has been a life filled with gentle formation and trial by fire, for him and for those who shared his journey.

Young men and women of all races, religions, and backgrounds have benefitted from his empathy and the look in his eyes that says, "I know and understand you." Adults have benefited as well, which I can attest to as both a staff member and friend for nearly two decades.

Parents, guardians, educators, and anyone who cares for children and the adults they will become, will be well served by Russell's "Si, Se Puede," ("Yes, you can") approach when interacting with kids. Russell has given students opportunities, disguised as alternative methods and solutions, to survive and thrive as "vessels" of hope for the generations that follow.

Former Co-Worker

Evolution. My life has been blessed in many ways, one of which was meeting and working with Russell Morrow. I was a late-hire, as a Special Education teacher, and was placed on an Alternative Education campus where Russell was the Principal. We dealt with middle school and high school students who had been expelled from their neighborhood schools.

While not under Russell's direct supervision, he became my mentor and support person. He guided me through the initial introductions to staff, the learning of the culture of the school, and how to best utilize the talents of all staff members. Joining an experienced staff that had worked together, and trusted one another, can be difficult, but Russell made the transition almost seamless.

The times when I did get frustrated, with either students or staff, Russell was my sounding board. He calmly listened, asked clarifying questions, and discussed the consequences of each possible solution I proposed. He was never judgmental, instead offering insights based on his years of experience, which allowed me to prosper.

As he got to know me better, Russell offered one insightful comment that I remember daily. "Some people see the world in black and white. You see it in kaleidoscope." That one statement has had a profound impact on all my relationships since.

As you will no doubt conclude after reading this book: Isn't it amazing how 7th grade boys evolve! Enjoy!

Former Co-Worker

Acknowledgements

Initially, the reader must understand that the following narrative is not meant as a definitive, psychological thesis about the titled group of students. This semi-autobiographical description and depiction of the 7th grade immature boy is based solely on my personal experiences and is meant only to offer parents and school personnel insights into the mindset of this child/student. This book was written from an educational perspective and the title selected only in humor and to be eye-catching.

Thanks must first go to the students, parents, and co-workers who provided some of my stories, which validated that I was not the only 7th grade boy who passed through and survived the "immature" years. While many friends and peers in my adult years questioned my sanity for working with middle school students, I thoroughly enjoyed my years with them and with the dedicated staffs that also enjoyed their tenure with this age group.

There were many students who did not fit the title description, of course, and I want to acknowledge them and their parents, as well.

A second thank you must go to my wife. Somehow, at a very early age, Mandy saw the potential in me that was not readily seen by others. As she states, "When we were married, I was 20 going on 30, and Russell was 20 going on 16!" As this statement suggests, "immature 7th grade boys" often take longer to attain full maturity, whether psychological, physical, or social. She has provided a level of understanding, encouragement, and loving guidance throughout our years together that was critical to my maturation process and productive life as a husband, parent and educator. I have been truly blessed to have her in my life and am eternally grateful for her love and, yes, patience!

As we pass through our lives, we usually meet others who have had positive impacts upon us, as well. I will attempt to show my undying gratitude for them as I write this narrative, to honor and recognize the assistance I was blessed to receive from them.

I want to thank my illustrator, Jan Harston. I first met Jan while vacationing in northern California. I dropped into her art studio and was immediately struck by her artistic talents, her creativity, and her sense of life and wonderment. She remains a respected confidant and dear friend.

Jan has been able to fully immerse herself in her passion for art since her retirement as a middle school secretary (How is that for good Karma!) and we remain the best of friends and supporters of each other, even though separated by hundreds of miles.

Lastly, my former students will finally have the answer to their oft-asked question, "Mr. Morrow, how do you always know what we're doing?"

Introduction

I was a Middle School teacher, Vice-Principal, and Principal for 32 of my 38 years in Education. As such, and as a self-proclaimed charter member of the title group, I have a very unique perspective into the inner workings of this group of students.

Just as I was always honest in working with my students, I will be brutally honest with the reader about my personal journey through, and beyond, this age group. I sincerely hope that the reader will be left with the knowledge that the vast majority of staff who work at the middle school level enjoys the challenge and relishes being first-hand observers to the educational, psychological, and physical maturity these students achieve.

All systems and vocational paths have their bad apples, of course, and Education is no exception. I have witnessed, and learned from those as well, but will address them only to compare them with the titled group of students. Learning what not to do, in any occupation, is just as important as learning what to do, as the judicial system, of course, can attest.

The reader needs to realize that growing up in the 1950s and '60s was much different than today. There was little to no fear of "stranger danger," "sex trafficking," or ministerial misconduct, then, so youngsters played freely until the street lights came on or the lightening bugs began to blink. We were encouraged to experience jobs early, whether babysitting, newspaper routes, or mowing lawns, for example. "Paperboys" and "altar boys" are the common references used here because, quite frankly, there were no girls performing in that capacity then.

Throughout this book are examples of my own youthful endeavors, which are shared in an effort to encourage parents and teachers of similar kids to never give up on them. The vast majority will improve in their dealings with others, will mature, will make you proud, and will live as productive and worthwhile citizens.

The names of the co-conspirators of my youth have been altered to protect them from events that might not have a statute of limitations!

Our own children are unaware of most of my personal shenanigans, and I am hopeful that our grandchildren will neither read nor hear of these experiences until they, too, have passed through this period of their lives.

Chapter 1

My Background

I really wasn't aware of how lucky I was to be raised as part of an intact family unit. With my two brothers and sister, our parents, the Air Force, our Catholic faith, sports, and the parochial schools we attended were major influences on our lives. As "Air Force people," our father was transferred often and we understood that new experiences and people were in our future.

Prior to meeting our mother, who served in the Women's Army Air Corps during WWII, dad was an airplane mechanic as a member of the, then called, Army Air Corps. Our father briefly worked in the public sector after the war but re-enlisted within a couple of years. While my older brother, sister, and I were all born in Detroit, Michigan, our younger brother was born in Germany.

Germany was our father's first deployment after the war and we were stationed there for four years, during my pre-school years. I attended Kindergarten though 3rd grades in Illinois, 4th grade in Texas, and 5th grade though the university level, both undergraduate and post-graduate studies, in Arizona. While in Arizona, our father retired as a Senior Master Sergeant after serving 22 years.

In addition to the parental duties and guidance our mother provided, she also worked outside our home. She possessed exemplary secretarial skills and worked first as a Secretary at a hospital and, then, at a local cannery.

Besides the gypsy life in the military and our dad's quick temper, our home lives were idyllic in our youth. As for our father's temper, he was raised and disciplined "by the switch," and continued that "tradition" as his first form of discipline and as he deemed necessary.

My brothers and I were all altar boys at church on Sundays and I was selected often to serve at wedding and funeral services. While looking angelic in the cassock, little did the church community suspect or know of my more mischievous side.

My older brother and I actually attended the seminary in high school, studying to become priests. While he stayed for three years, I left the seminary two-thirds of the way through my freshman year and as soon as I learned the meaning of "celibacy." Having been taught by nuns my entire elementary school years, this was another definition of "none" that I was not enamored by!

I learned very early the value of the dollar and the hard work required to earn it. I had a TV Guide route while in Texas and my older brother and I had paper routes in Arizona. I delivered, by bike, a regional paper during 5th grade and the local paper during 6th grade.

The regional paper was delivered seven days a week, including a Sunday edition, which required us to be at work by 3:30 AM, so our customers had their morning papers by 6 AM. There was really only one delivery I fretted over on those early Sunday mornings, one that was off a very dark alley behind an apartment complex and abutted the railroad tracks through town. We did have a few "hobos" back then and I was fearful of that particular group.

An important part of the TV Guide and paper routes was the monthly duty of "collecting" the price of each subscription from our customers. While delivering or collecting, paperboys were encouraged to add more customers to our routes, through the bi-monthly contests that awarded prizes to the ones for the most new "starts."

I got to know several residents of that apartment complex, who weren't my steady customers, during the delivery and collection process, as my usual customers introduced us. Whenever a contest occurred, several of those tenants would purchase the paper from me for one month so I might win the contest. I utilized this "gold mine" of new subscribers often, which helped me to win various prizes including trips to amusement parks, movie sets, and sporting events. While "collecting," I often received monthly tips from many of my customers, which was in addition to my regular salary, for always throwing their papers onto their porches and for my courteous demeanor.

I was never shy about knocking on strangers' doors seeking new subscriptions, as I had a spiel ready for the adult with whom I would be speaking. Additionally, dad had purchased a little printing press he thought my older brother and I should have for our first endeavor into the "business world." We made personal business cards to deliver to our patrons and possible future patrons, as we sought to expand our routes.

One particular "start" I was most proud of occurred one evening when I approached, what to me, was almost a mansion. The owner declined my offer to subscribe to the regional paper, explaining that he was the editor of local competition. Before walking away, however, I suggested he take the "Sunday only" subscription, as I knew that his paper did not deliver on Sundays. As stated, I was not shy and the editor did subscribe for the "Sunday only" subscription for one month. He also invited me to come to work at his paper, saying that he wished all of his paperboys were as diligent and convincing.

I met this editor a year later when we moved within town and a route for his paper opened up right in my neighborhood. He recognized me at the office building one day and was glad to have me as a paperboy for his paper. Believe me, I was just as glad to work for his paper, as I no longer had to rise at 3AM on Sundays!

I must have been just as angelic-looking without the cassock worn by altar boys, as the editor selected me to adorn the front page of the paper, holding a sparkler for a July 4th edition.

Baseball, both in and outside of school, was the sport of choice for my brothers and me, while our sister played field hockey at school. As we graduated to high school, my younger brother and I also played basketball and football. From this small high school, we each received Most Valuable Player awards in our respective senior years, providing further evidence of our diligence to pursue our goals.

Also in my senior year, I was introduced to formal music through my involvement in a mixed chorus, called "Glee Club." While my grades in school were average, at best, I was selected as President of the Glee Club, experiencing my first leadership position. In addition to keeping the class on task whenever Sister Christine was called from class, the main responsibility was giving an introductory speech at our Christmas performance, my initial public speaking experience. Little did I know then that I would continue singing with church choirs until the age of seventy-one and that my chosen vocation would require public speaking on a daily basis.

Using myself as a primary example throughout this narrative, and after causing my parents and teachers much aggravation, I did graduate from college with a major in Physical Education and a minor in History. I also achieved advanced degrees, as I began working in Education. As I walked across the various stages, I'm certain some of the nuns that taught me were spinning over in their graves in utter and total disbelief!

I started my teaching and coaching career, at age 22, at a small rural elementary school, that had a largely Hispanic and migratory student population. The school was situated in southern Arizona, surrounded by field crops of lettuce, cotton, and cantaloupes that our students' parents labored in. Over half of the families spent much of December and January in Mexico, fixing up their permanent homes and visiting with relatives. Some made the circuitous route to Mexico and, then, to Texas before returning to Arizona. Several also left for the California fields during April or May. The other one-third, who remained in the area, consisted of the children of the landowners and the families of foremen on the farms.

I taught at the elementary school from 1970-78; being the homeroom teacher at 6th grade for 4 years, 7th grade for 3 years, and the 8th grade for 1 year. While there I began coaching as well. I coached a variety of sports throughout my career, both in and outside of school, and after I retired in 2008. That little school of about 250 students was the hub of the community; offering periodic band performances, Christmas plays, and occasional health presentations. Each of these events was preceded by delicious potluck dinners enthusiastically provided by our PTA parents. Unfortunately, that elementary school has since closed and students from the area are now bussed to communities 10-15 miles away.

In my early thirties, I worked 5 years as a Career Counselor at a county office of education in northern Arizona. I taught high school students enrolled in our vocational classes, on five different campuses, the art of writing resumes and preparing for interviews. I also provided some students with "Job-Shadowing" experiences and assisted many to complete college or vocational school applications. At the conclusion of each school year my duties also included working at the county fair; organizing all of the vocational exhibits for our woodworking and welding classes and the skill contests for typing, welding, and auto mechanics students.

While in this position, I was able to complete my Counseling Credential requirements, during the summers, and my Arizona Administrative Credential and Master's Degree at a nearby university.

From 1983 to 1991, I returned to the traditional public school sector in a far northern and remote part of Arizona; one year as a high school Counselor and then as the Vice-Principal at the local middle school for seven years. As Vice-Principal, I was in charge of student discipline and, even though in my administrative capacity, sometimes coached the 7th grade boys' or girls' basketball teams.

For the last 18 years of my career we moved back to southern Arizona, to be closer to my ailing father, and to accept Principal positions; first at a medium sized middle school, serving 600-700 students, and, then, in a combined Principal position as the Principal of a Community School and Principal of the county's Juvenile Hall.

As the Principal of the middle school for 10 years I was, again, chief disciplinarian as well as the instructional leader. In the latter position I lead the staffs in dealing with middle and high school students who had, for the most part, been expelled from their local school systems. While still the chief disciplinarian at the community school, the juvenile hall correctional officers had that responsibility for those housed in their facility.

Chapter 2

Characteristics of the Immature Male Student

Although the title characters usually progressed to middle school with some history of minor disciplinary problems, their reputation as a trouble-causing student was fully developed at the middle school level. While most students at the middle school level begin noticeable bodily changes, the immature boy may not experience the same for months, or even years, later.

The immature 7th grade boy is usually one of the shortest, if not the shortest, in his class. Usually, he is only shoulder height to the girls and the more mature boys, as the others have already begun the physical maturation process. Being self-conscious about his lack of physical growth, he will also illustrate his resultant lack of self-confidence by, almost constantly, trying to prove himself to others.

Despite the widely held belief that he is seeking attention through his antics, in reality he is seeking acceptance from his classmates and friends. He will use his sense of humor, his innate intelligence, his well-honed observation skills, and his willingness to take risks as tools to attain this acceptance. These acceptance-getting activities aren't reserved for the school setting and are in evidence at home and in the community, as well.

After an "event" that this student might participate in, parents, teachers, administrators, neighbors, and, sometimes, police officers will often ask, "What on earth were you thinking?" That question is an absolutely fruitless endeavor to understand this student, and the honest answer is that he wasn't! Seeking and receiving acceptance takes precedence over the thought process or even of any possible consequences.

Other students and friends will sometimes seek out the immature one and suggest activities that they, themselves, would not do; for fear of getting caught or just exercising their good common sense that the immature one hasn't, yet, fully developed. Personally, there were a very few occasions in which I understood the others' fear and I wisely opted not to follow their suggestions. Other times, however, I took the challenge, was successful, and received even more of the desired acceptance from my peers.

The vast majority of these late-bloomers do mature and turn out to be good people and good citizens. A very few, however, seem to remain psychologically immature and continue to seek acceptance in immature, unacceptable, unforgivable, and, sometimes, illegal manners into their adult years. For the most part they end up in less successful life situations; most often resulting in divorce, alcohol or drug abuse, a spotty employment record, a criminal background or, sometimes, an early and untimely death.

The Here and Now

"Russell, do you know the part in the clothes washer that mixes everything up?" That was the opening question delivered by my mother, to me, after yet another melee with my older brother.

"Yes, ma'am. The agitator."

"That's exactly what you are, young man, the agitator. Why do you have to antagonize your older brother so much?"

While never spoken, 'That's my job' was on the tip of my tongue. Besides, he couldn't normally catch me and the everyday verbal jabs were my revenge for the times when the self-centered SOB did clobber me, usually in the evening and I was confined to a shared bedroom.

That I never once thought in advance to the time when we were confined together, before I verbally cut him to shreds and ran, speaks volumes of the immature, 7th grade boys' mindset. The 'here and now' concept prevails and, hardly ever, the down-the-road-reality of future consequences. Unfortunately, this general lapse of good judgment wasn't confined to the home, much to the chagrin of the nuns at school and parents, friends, neighbors, and classmates in all other social settings.

"Russell is not working up to his potential" was a comment on numerous quarterly report cards, up through my sophomore year of high school. That comment was written so often, and by so many different nuns, that it completely lost any significance to me by the 7th grade. The 'here and now' mindset was so dead set, in this single case, in not being noticed by the nuns that no extra effort was made on my part for their acceptance. I had witnessed the cruelty and delight some of the nuns had in dispensing corporal punishments, that I kept my head and hands down, spending my time, instead, doodling and dreaming about recess, girls, and after school sports and activities. My grades, while passing, reflected my general lack of interest in schoolwork and in pleasing the nuns.

It should be noted here, that requiring a C average in high school for extracurricular activities was a positive incentive for me! While I kept my grades up well enough to participate in sports at the high school level, I didn't really begin to seriously put forth full effort and attention to my studies until marriage at age 20 and in my senior year in college.

Most of my creative endeavors to seek acceptance occurred after school and out in the community. Cutting into a neighbor's watermelon; stealing Christmas lights off neighboring houses; dismantling safety signs for the marbles within; egging cars at Halloween; and, breaking windows at the local public school were examples of the 'here and now' thinking that, if caught, led to some form of corporal punishment. That these punishments were sometimes humiliating and painful had not one iota of impact nor recognition to the 'here and now' brain of this immature boy! Nor will it have any impact on your child/student at this level of immaturity. The 'here and now' simply outweighs all other concerns and possible consequences.

I learned very early on, however, that when faced with the fact that your parents already knew you had done something wrong, the best policy was to confess quickly. I was impetuous, yes, but I wasn't stupid! This was the case with the neighbor's watermelon, throwing eggs, and Christmas lights.

Dad was a military man and used whatever was handy to ply out some righteous punishment on my butt; be it his own huge hands, a belt, or a slipper. I knew I was going to get it and that I deserved it, but at least admitting my guilt seemed to lessen the length of the punishment and the subsequent pain. The 'here and now' mind set occasionally told me that it was fruitless to deny my act, feign innocence, or lie about extenuating circumstances.

The absolute height of the 'here and now' phenomenon was after my last whipping when I looked over my shoulder at my father and asked, "Is that all you've got?" And, no, it wasn't!

While my parents were wise to some of my extra-curricular activities, many went undiscovered and were only shared with peers.

Intelligence

Even though these boys don't perform academically at their best, they do possess an innate intelligence and creativity that fuels their pranks. Their creativity is on display at all times, as they contemplate how to gain the desired acceptance from their peers. After all, where is the fun or recognition in studying and getting good grades?

In my case, my hidden intelligence was enhanced by my observation and listening skills. I could have done better, but I did not want any attention from the nuns. Even though I was listening, I offered neither opinions nor answers and never studied too hard for tests, quizzes, or essays.

Over the years, I had witnessed other students getting their hands slapped with rulers, being head-slapped from behind, and, once, even thrown back into the desk so hard that the desk toppled over with the student still in the attached seat! Neither positive nor negative recognition or acceptance from the nuns was my goal and I was quite successful at that through my sophomore year of high school.

Quick Learners

Being from a military family and moving often, gaining acceptance of my peers was extremely important.

My earliest recollection of being somewhat of a deviously quick learner was in the 4th grade in Texas. Within the first week, I noticed that the custodian had the duty of collecting five cents from anyone who wanted to purchase a soda during lunch. He was also charged with watching the students in the cafeteria, so his attention was divided. The custodian kept an ever-growing palm full of nickels but spent most of his time observing the other students.

I decided to keep my nickel while I tickled the other coins, making the custodian think I had actually paid. I kept a nickel in my hand just in case he emptied his palm before I got to the front of the line, which was very rare. I don't remember paying over twenty-five cents over the course of the entire year, whenever I wanted a soda instead of the milk that came with the meal!

As part of gaining peer acceptance, I shared this technique with my closest friends and tablemates. While disbelieving at first, I emptied my pockets one day of all change but kept just one nickel. When I returned to the table with my nickel and soda in hand, I had earned the acceptance I so desired. Some of the others also developed the nerve and learned to be successful in this endeavor, as well.

The nun I had as a classroom teacher during the 4th grade raffled off a monthly prize for those who made donations to the poor. As you made your donation, you also completed a raffle entry with your name on it. No one ever realized that I was stuffing the box with raffle entries every other month, as I was bright enough not to do this every month and draw undue attention to myself. Even though I won the prize every other month because of my "generosity," my deviousness went unnoticed and undiscovered.

Early in the 7th grade, Kevin, Patrick, and I were in the restroom at the same time. We found great joy in wetting paper towels and throwing them to stick on the ceiling and walls. Perfectly exhibiting the power of the 'here and now' concept, we were not quiet about it and one of the nuns from a nearby classroom called the Principal.

Sister Margaret, an old and very ugly nun in the eyes of this 7th grader, stormed into the restroom while I was at the urinal. She proceeded to rant and rave about the damages and demanded to know which of us had been involved. She went to us, one by one, bending over to within a foot of our eyes, and demanded to know if we, specifically, had partaken in the antics.

When she came to me, I denied any involvement and reminded her that I had my hands full (that might have been a slight exaggeration as I was still "immature" in several ways) at the urinal when she arrived. She bent even closer to me, within an inch, staring me directly in the eyes, and asked again if I was involved.

From that moment on, until she was transferred three years later, I owned her! I immediately understood that if I could look an ugly, old crone directly in the eyes without blinking or flinching, I could tell her anything. And, after all, I had a military father at home that could beat my butt raw, so staring a wretched old nun down while lying to her was going to be a piece of cake!

This new knowledge was utilized throughout her remaining tenure and effectively saved me while stealing candy from the school store, sipping on the wine and eating some of the communion wafers after mass, and copying some Algebra homework during my freshman year.

Luckily, she was replaced my junior year of high school, by Sister Agnes, who actually enjoyed her students! Sister Agnes changed the culture of the school, and my less than favorable feelings toward a Principal and towards nuns in general.

Hypersensitivity

These boys are so determined to gain acceptance that any serious slight is taken personally and shakes them to their core. Whether at home, in school, or in the community, and already self-conscious about their "short comings," whatever is perceived as a serious insult is met by withdrawal and more negative self-doubt.

Singing along with the music on the radio was a favorite pastime of mine, from a very early age. My parents, hearing this constantly, attempted to encourage my singing by purchasing a guitar for me from the local music store.

Calling all of us for dinner, I was interrupted one evening as I was singing along to a song and strumming my guitar. Dad walked into our room unannounced, and seeing what I was doing, giggled slightly and closed the door. Feeling quite devastated by my father's reaction, I never picked up the guitar again, until I sold it to a classmate 4 years later.

School staff will observe the same response from their students and must be cognizant of possible negative reactions, up to and including suicide, unfortunately. An event at home may carryover to school, and vice versa, so communication between the home and school is imperative.

Chapter 3

The Christmas Caper

Undeniably, the best example of the 'here and now' and quick thinking

was during a very mild 7th grade Christmas season in the southern valley

of Arizona, when I spent an overnight stay on the military base with good friend, Thomas. Thomas actually lived and attended school in another community and one would naturally assume that we wouldn't even know each other. Being from military families, however, Thomas and I had originally met in Illinois, when both of our fathers were stationed there.

On the night I stayed with Thomas it was so warm that we actually camped out in the back yard! We decided that night to cruise the base housing on foot and see what was going on.

At some point, we decided to harass the carolers and others. Christmas lights were furtively removed from around the fronts of houses, and hurtled at the carolers during their performances. An empty soda bottle was launched close to a lady carrying her clean laundry home, scaring her to death, and resulting in her laundry being scattered around a 5 to 10-foot circumference. A bonfire was built behind the rear tire of one person's car and a small mailbox was propped open and the contents lit on fire. Additional Christmas lights were heaved onto the main access road to the base housing, in front of cars driving by. We were lucky that no one crashed, even as we enjoyed the drivers' temporary shock and the resultant swerving.

In the morning, Thomas and I decided to peruse the area and see if our shenanigans had been noticed. We kept walking when we noticed MPs (Military Police) taking a report from the owner of the car whose back tire was burned and flat. We also kept walking past more MPs, who were investigating a burned out mailbox. Because I had been caught throwing

Christmas lights the night before, and might be recognized, we decided to discontinue looking at all of our handiwork.

Immediately upon my arrival home, though, my father took me aside and asked, "Was that you and Thomas that created all that havoc last night?" When I admitted it, my dad informed me that, "every single car moving around last night was an off-duty MP looking for you two criminals."

I was sent to my room while my father called Thomas' father. While certainly deserved, I don't remember my punishment being all that bad and, I am sure, partly because I owned up to the escapades immediately. The disappointment in my parents' faces was enough, in this case, to make me stop and think. Thomas, though, went out the next year and did the same types of pranks again!

I have no idea whatever happened to Thomas, as his family was transferred during his 8th grade year.

This caper was not, however, without a close call of being caught and turned into the authorities.

An adult, whose family was being caroled to, decided to chase Thomas and me after an onslaught of Christmas lights. We naturally knew to split up but, upon being caught and questioned, the NCO (Non-commissioned Officer) asked my name. I, of course, immediately gave him the name of another 7th grade boy in my class. When asked who my partner was, I gave the name of, yet, another classmate of mine. By pure happenstance, the last name I selected for Thomas was the same last name of the base commander at the time. When asked, again at very close range, if that was "General Samuel's" son, I replied while staring him directly in the eyes, without blinking or a moment's hesitation, "I'm not sure of his rank, sir." Not wanting a possible confrontation with the base commander, the NCO directed me to return later and clean up the mess. 'No way in hell' was my only thought as I raced away, found Thomas, and returned to finish our night of camping.

Chapter 4

Feeding the Sweet Tooth

As stated earlier, the antics of the immature 7th grade boy usually begin at an earlier age. Another preliminary shenanigan that perfectly illustrates all the characteristics of these students occurred during the summer between 5th and 6th grades.

In the late 1950s and early 1960s, glass soda bottles were returned to grocery stores for a small refund; usually three cents per bottle. Most of my salary and tips from delivering papers was placed into a savings account, so I also collected bottles and saved the proceeds until I could afford to purchase candy. As this took some time, however, I often just stole the candy I wanted.

While at the grocery store one day, I saw a patron return an empty wooden container that normally held twenty-four soda bottles. When I saw the clerk return three dollars to the customer, I immediately plotted a new way to purchase candy and feed my sweet tooth.

The grocery store owner kept these valuable soda containers behind the store, within a locked 10-foot fence. It was very easy to scale that fence at dusk, steal a container, turn it back into the same grocery store the next day, and "purchase" all the candy I wanted. Ingenious!

During my freshman and sophomore years in high school, I still had a demanding sweet tooth, which was easily fed by volunteering to sell from the student store during lunch recess. Chocolate covered mints were my favorite and were easily pocketed, even in the presence of two or three other students. Yes, Sister Margaret did question me, but to no avail.

I must have been developing some sense of guilt by that time in my life, however, and did attempt to track the number of items I took and repay that amount at the beginning of the next month. Summer jobs later provided me with enough money so that I actually bought the candy the last two years of high school.

Chapter 5

Classmates and Friends

Playing marbles was a big playground activity at school in the late 1950s and early 1960s. It was Kevin who first introduced me to dismantling traffic signs, like "Yield" signs or ones with directional arrows, for the red marbles that acted as the reflectors at night. We stole them from the entrances to the nearby Jr. High school; never, of course, thinking about the safety reasons for their installation. While the other students were spending their allowances at the local department store for their marbles, our creative activity gave Kevin and me free and easy access to ammunition for these games.

Kevin and I also were involved together in discovering and eating chunks out of a neighbor's watermelon. Since we didn't eat too much, we thought we were being clever in turning the watermelon over so the resultant hole couldn't be seen. We found out within two days, though, that the watermelon was being raised for the annual County Fair competition! This ended up being just one more example of the 'here and now' thinking, and also resulted in a butt whipping and the confiscation of the knife I had received the prior Christmas.

While not resulting in any damages to either our person or losses to neighbors, Kevin and I also went around the neighborhood that summer knocking down wasp nests from local houses, trees, and garages. I, somehow, knew that if we remained still after knocking down the nests, we would never get stung. We remained static while the wasps buzzed around us for about 5 minutes and, then, were able to pick up our valued nest and add it to the collection we kept in my parents' garage. By the end of that summer, we had between 80 and 100 wasp nests of various sizes and shapes. I'm positive that our parents and local residents were questioning our sanity all the while we added to our collection of nests.

We laughed heartily, though, when two separate neighborhood adults refused to let us knock down the nests around their houses. Both were stung at least 3 times before they got inside their front doors! Kevin and

I just waited the requisite 5 minutes and added even more nests to our summer collection.

Although Kevin continued his antics at the local public high school, he eventually matured and worked successfully, it turned out, in the criminal justice system.

Raymond

As 7th graders, in addition to playing marbles, a lunchtime activity included a game known as "chicken." In it, one boy climbed on the back of another and they tried to knock down the other teams of players. The last team standing won the game and was declared the winners. As I was one of the smallest in my class, it made perfectly good sense to me to select the largest boy, Raymond, as my partner. Raymond was also seeking acceptance from our classmates, as he was often the butt of jokes regarding his weight, and readily agreed to this partnership.

That we won this game almost daily did bring about a strategy from the others that resulted in a broken collarbone for me. The other teams devised a scheme to attack us from all sides at once. Unfortunately, the team behind us hit us first and the others toppled on top. The resultant broken bone also resulted in the banning of this game by the nuns. While that game ended, it did provide us the acceptance both Raymond and I were seeking.

While no longer able to gain recognition and acceptance from this game, I do remember antagonizing my other classmates at lunch recess during my recuperation. No one, of course, wanted to hurt me again so I harassed and ran for the next month or so.

After healing, though, one incident of retribution by the others ended this harassment for good. I was chased into the boys' restroom by several of my classmates, where I was stripped down to my underwear, in an effort to have me fully comprehend that I would no longer get away with the harassment I had dealt out while injured. Being the quick learner that I was, all harassment and antics towards them ceased immediately.

Well, that, and the threat that they would make me retrieve my pants outside of the restroom the next time helped just a little!

Joe

Joe was a teammate on a local Pony League baseball team for two summers and attended the local public junior high. During those two summers after 7th and 8th grades, however, we also initiated attempts at smoking, sipping alcohol, and playing in the local creek. As my father was an addicted smoker, however, I found the taste and smell of tobacco abhorrent and never continued.

Drinking alcohol was a different matter, all together. One of us would sneak a little alcohol from whatever bottle was open in one of our houses. While my parents' drink of choice was bourbon, Joe and I also sampled gin, vodka, and beer that he had confiscated, in either his back yard or at a creek that ran through our community.

In addition to the swimming and experimenting with alcohol at the creek, Joe and I enjoyed jumping from a railroad trestle to the water below. The most fun was jumping from the trestle when a passenger train passed by. We absolutely loved the startled look on the faces of the passengers as we first jumped skyward and waved, before dropping into the waters below!

Joe, unfortunately, was killed a few years later in Vietnam.

Patrick

Patrick was another neighborhood friend and we spent a lot of time playing sports and riding bikes. He was at least a foot taller than me in the 7th grade, but let me tag along and participate in most of his activities. From pick-up tackle football games during the weekends and to baseball and dove hunting during those seasons, we had a good, and usually safe, time.

During the evenings, however, no matter what time of year, we enjoyed harassing the neighbors. Ringing doorbells was a favorite pastime and we were experts at never being caught. We had some adults search around their homes and walk the streets looking for us, to no avail, as we were quite adept at hiding under cars or climbing trees. Watching and quietly snickering while they searched seemed to bring the most enjoyment. Other activities included stealing Christmas lights, toilet-papering houses, and egging cars.

As I was quite naïve, it was Patrick who introduced me to "adult magazines" one summer. I was amazed there were such magazines and it was Patrick who also explained about the "Birds and the Bees," as neither my parents nor the nuns ever spoke about the maturation process or of sexual matters.

Sex originally came up as Patrick and I were walking the fence between his house and a neighbor's one evening. We passed by his bathroom window only to glimpse his older sister getting out of the shower.

"Wow!"

Patrick laughed and pushed me further along the fence, realizing just how truly naïve I was. He and our mutual friends had several good laughs at my expense, but I was getting acceptance as part of the group, so I didn't mind. As I had been working on the mysteries of sex with nary a clue, Patrick continued the discussions about girls and sex throughout that memorable summer.

Patrick was another classmate that left the parochial elementary school to attend the public high school in town. He continued his pranks in high school, but worked and retired successfully from a variety of municipal positions in the communities in which he resided.

The Three Amigos Plus One

As this suggests, these friends tolerated me and allowed me to tag along often. While Buck and Andy began school together in Kindergarten, I arrived at the parochial school in the 5th grade and Bill arrived in the 7th. Again, pick-up games of football, basketball, and baseball were the highlights in our youth, whatever the time of the year.

In addition to just tagging along, I also tried to make myself useful to the other amigos. While climbing the rooftops of the local public high school one day, we discovered an open window into the school gymnasium. I offered to attempt to squeeze through the opening, was successful, and we enjoyed many days and evenings after that, playing basketball in the relative coolness of the gym.

I introduced the trio to sampling the wine after mass services, as well. Whether at the main church downtown or at our school's multipurpose room, I had noticed that the priests usually changed out of their vestments and exited quickly. As clearing the altar was one of the tasks of the altar boys, the imbibing of the wine and swallowing a few more hosts was easy to do. I think the priests must have paid $1 for a truckload of the wine, as it was "God-awful!"

We had to be a little more careful at school, of course, as the "evil" Sister Margaret was always on alert and ready, willing, and able to dish out whatever punishment she thought was deserved for anything she considered inappropriate.

Lest the reader get the impression that Sister Margaret was only looking to discipline the boys, girls suffered as well. Mini-skirts were in fashion in the early 60's and all the girls had to kneel before her to make sure their skirts touched the floor. The girls became very adept at rolling up or rolling down their skirts, as needed. Additionally, their blouses all had to have sleeves, and the few blondes had to be checked to make sure their roots were not showing! I'll leave the rationale for these behaviors up to the imagination of the reader!

When the "amigos" got together in the evenings to listen to music or play board games, I regaled them with stories of my other antics. "Oh, Russell!" was not an uncommon refrain.

As we got older and began to drive, we attended local dances together, as well. While I had learned some of the mysteries about girls and dating from Patrick, the Amigos were almost completely clueless! When Buck walked away from a girl he had danced with only once, I took an interest and started dancing with her. We danced the rest of the evening together and celebrated our 50th Anniversary in August of 2018! I don't remember any of the others dating at all during high school.

Buck and Andy both attended different high schools, while Bill and I continued at our local parochial school through our senior year.

The four of us remained close, however, and worked and played together during the summers. All through and after high school, we held summer jobs in a tomato shed and, after reaching 18, at a cannery. I actually lied about my age on the application form for the cannery and began working there at 17. As my mother was, by then, working as the secretary in the warehouse, her boss and the main office staff turned a blind eye when I claimed to be 18.

While we had already experimented with a little alcohol after mass, we began to imbibe more often as we progressed in high school. Other, older looking students purchased the beer for us throughout our junior year of high school.

During our senior year of high school, and afterwards, Andy purchased the beer. At about 6'5," he passed for much older and had no problem at the local liquor store in purchasing.

Since my parents were chaperoning a local dance on New Year's Eve, in our senior year of high school, Andy bought some beer and the four of us returned to my house to share the two six-packs. Bill only had two beers but was already throwing up before we arrived at the dance. I had four beers and had to urinate about every 10 minutes while we drove around town before attending the dance. I probably took too much pleasure when one of the stops we made was in front of the nuns' convent!

Those frequent stops should have been an omen to me about future drinking, but I was still in the midst of the 'here and now' mindset, even in high school. My parents wondered why I was making frequent trips to the restroom at the dance, but never discerned, nor asked, the reason.

Bill and I had one memorable drinking incident later on in the school year, though. As Bill was restricted to driving 50 miles a week, I was usually the driver while we "cruised main." We were at another classmate's house, afterwards, when we began to drink hard liquor. This friend gave us some more, "for the road," and Bill and I found a quiet place a quarter-mile from my house to imbibe.

When Bill announced that he was feeling a little dizzy, we decided to stop by the local pool parlor to sober him up before I drove him home. While complaining of seeing double, he actually tore the felt on one table before we were asked to leave.

Upon arrival at his home, I watched him stagger up to the door and enter. He woke up the next morning in the bathtub, naked, and with his vomit-stained clothes on the floor. As part of Bill's punishment, I was never allowed to spend any more time with him without others being present. While the "others" were always Buck and Andy, however, this only limited Bill's drinking endeavors, as he didn't want another "bath tub incident."

Andy continued to buy our beer when we worked the night shift at the cannery. As all of us had college plans, we decided to work the night shift as workers earned ten cents more an hour than the day shift and also had the opportunity to work a couple of overtime hours. A small ice chest was hidden in the weeds some evenings and provided cool refreshment at lunch break during those hot and humid summer nights.

During our first summer at the cannery, we each had different jobs. Mine was replacing and emptying the "pie pans" for the ladies who were sorting the fruit, taking the ones in the worst shape from the belt and placing the into their pans. Upon inquiring about why the pans were called "pie pans," I was informed that the damaged fruit was set aside to make frozen pies or small snack pies.

After working several summers at the cannery, I have yet to partake of any frozen or snack pies!

The following summers, we all worked together in the warehouse, where the two-hour shifts were divided among a variety of tasks; from the simplicity of adding cardboard fiber between stacks of the canned fruit, to loading of boxcars with heavy boxes of the desired quantities and sizes of the fruit cans.

My last summer working at the cannery was highlighted by an accident I had while performing overtime. The duty involved cleaning the conveyer belts that carried the fruit past the sorters, so the day shift had a clean surface the next morning. My brush got caught in between the moving belt and the side railing. Before I could pull it free, the brush was pulled under an electrical box and the box exploded.

As I explained to my mother before the next evening's shift, it was either break my arm under the same electrical box or let the brush continue. Yes, my hidden intelligence told me to save my arm, first! It was then that my mother explained that the entire half of the cannery was going to be shut down for three weeks while the electrical panel was repaired and moved. She had spent her entire workday calling employees to let them know their jobs were temporarily stopped. Needless to say, I never worked another overtime shift!

The three amigos were definitely the more mature among this cadre, with me lagging behind in that category and, also, in our school studies. While all three were accepted into universities directly from high school, my college career started at the local junior college, before transferring to a nearby state college.

They earned degrees in Pre-Med, Social Work, and Physics, respectfully, and each has had successful careers, became model citizens, and good human beings. We remained good friends over several years, attending professional or college sporting events to maintain contact.

Chapter 6

Some Students

Alfonso was a member of the largest class in the history of the rural school where I first taught. The class was large enough that the lowest students, as determined by yearly academic testing, were always teamed with the smaller class behind them. This went on from the primary grades until I got them in the 7th grade. (Can you say, Karma?)

This group of students had the same boring teacher, also, as they progressed from 2nd through 6th grades. While the rationale was that these students would benefit by having the material repeated, they only became rowdier and more disruptive each year. As I had heard Mr. Bennett speak in the teachers' lounge and at staff meetings in the same monotone voice, I could only imagine the boredom these students faced for five long, agonizing years. I also, quite frankly, wondered how on earth he managed to keep his job!

When this class entered the 7th grade, I asked the Principal/ Superintendent to please combine all the kids together in my homeroom. As they were entering a departmentalized program at the Jr. High level, I was their teacher for Language Arts, History, and Physical Education. Their prior teacher also became part of the departmentalized team of teachers, teaching Science to all the 7th and 8th grade classes.

It was painfully obvious within a day or two, that the students who had Mr. Bennett for those years were sadly deficient in their Reading and Comprehension skills and would be bored to death with the teaching methods that were successfully used with prior classes. Within a week, I made a big production of throwing away the History textbooks, which concentrated on the study of European countries, as most had difficulty reading and understanding the text anyway. When they went out to morning recess, I collected the texts from the garbage can and locked them inside one of the classroom cabinets for the remainder of the year.

The students, then, began to learn how to format letters, and sent requests to various European Embassies for information. All waited anxiously to receiving mail at the school from their respective countries and began to study and learn about their selected country, its history, and current events! Student reports, utilizing the information received and studied, were prepared for presentations before their classmates and, then, for their parents at Open House.

Basic reading and vocabulary skills were taught by me and emphasized peer teaching by the more advanced students. This was a win-win situation as the lower academic students weren't being lectured to and the higher academic students received reinforcement skills by having to learn the material well enough to teach it. This teaching method was utilized in all subjects, as well, upon the migratory students' return from their winter hiatus in Mexico or Texas. Bi-lingual students were assigned as "learning buddies" whenever a non-English speaking student arrived in our classes.

It doesn't take a genius to figure out that a class this deficient in reading and math skills, and one that had the same boring teacher for five straight years, would gravitate toward being disruptive and defiant. They actually took pride and honor in this reputation as they entered the middle school program. Even though their behavior improved dramatically during their 7th grade, their well-earned reputation preceded them and the 8th grade teacher and I exchanged homeroom grade levels the next year.

The chief proponent of this misbehavior was Alfonso. While I am proud to say that the class averaged almost five years of academic growth in the two years I had them, Alfonso continued to challenge his teachers, including me, whenever he could.

As an example, during the first week of 7th grade, Alfonso informed me that he could get the aforementioned, Mr. Bennett, screaming at the class within 20 minutes of the next period. In my disbelief at this statement, Alfonso said he would knock on the adjoining wall when he was successful. Not caring to know exactly how he did it, at 20 minutes into the class, I heard Mr. Bennett screaming at the top of his lungs and Alfonso's predictive knock on the wall!

If Alfonso had spent as much time studying as he did in getting under his teachers' skins, he would have been a very fine student. Yeah, yeah...Alfonso was "not working up to his potential" either but I was determined to have a positive impact on him and the others that were in the departmentalized program. His behavior did improve, as did his grades, when I got him involved in the football, basketball, track, and baseball teams I coached at the school.

I was not immune to Alfonso's antics, however, and he illustrated his personal intelligence and power of observation through his misbehaviors. As a precursor to this story, I must admit to having a nightmarish incident involving my pants zipper while dating in high school. To this day, I double-check my zipper before going out in public or to participate in a public forum.

While in front of the class or while checking on student progress, Alfonso quickly learned that if he looked down toward my zipper, I would make haste to the podium I kept at the front of the classroom to, quickly and without notice, double check my zipper. It wasn't until half the year was over, and one of the male students was presenting his

Social Studies report, that I realized there was a five-inch gap between the top portion of the podium and the body of the podium…right at zipper level! Much to my chagrin, I realized then that the entire class was aware of my quirk and fully watched me check my zipper every time I did so. Quite frankly, I had met my match; Alfonso was the new and improved "agitator!"

Alfonso has married and raised his family in the nearby community, and has enjoyed a successful career as a truck driver.

Julio

Julio was innocent looking enough; a bear cub shaped body, huge brown eyes with a seemingly constant glint, full face and cheeks, and two gold-capped front teeth. Just as this author, Julio was also one of the shortest males in his class and did whatever he needed to do in order to gain the acceptance of his peers.

Julio's primary ploy for gaining acceptance was evident within the first 10 minutes of being in my classroom! While taking roll, in my initial attempt to place names with faces, Julio piped in with student nicknames. Not once or twice, mind you, but after every single name. In unison, when I called Julio's name, the rest of the class chimed in with, "The Little Brown Bear." Those two gold-capped teeth glistened with pure delight from his proud grin.

Julio's ability to create an appropriate nickname was uncanny, as I learned throughout the year. I use the term "appropriate" very loosely as some, while being spot-on, were less than flattering and in today's world would not be tolerated and might border on harassment. As a small, country school, however, and in the early 1970's, the nicknames were accepted as they were intended; as Julio's attempt at both friendship and acceptance.

The tall, somewhat clumsy, thin boy was "Stork." The tall, thin girl was "the reed." All the others had names that reflected something unique about his or her body or demeanor. Ones I remember, included; "the pro" for the best athlete, "gabby", of course, for the quietest student, "oops" for the clumsiest, "Marilyn" for the only blonde girl, "ginger" for the redhead, and "riff-raff" for twin brothers who hardly ever arrived at school in clean clothes.

The challenge for me, of course, was to refer to each student by his or her given name and not by Julio's nicknames. While I was successful at doing this in the classroom, I have to admit to regaling the other staff members in the staff lounge with the nicknames and other "Julio-isms" throughout the year.

Julio had to be reeled in about once a month, as his attempts to gain acceptance could get under an occasional collar or broach on the inappropriate. Luckily for me, Julio could be reined in with just a look, which he understood innately, and easily apologized when necessary. He was also one of the very bright students in his class and could be counted upon to provide insight that enhanced most discussions or assist in the tutorial sessions when students returned from the annual winter hiatus.

Julio never returned for his 8th grade year and I have no idea of what has happened to him.

Chapter 7

Earned Respect

While the great majority of our students came from very poor farm-working families, with over half of the students being migratory as their parents followed the crops, these mainly Hispanic children always arrived at school clean and in clean clothing. Many lived in less than ideal housing, some even at an old WWII training base nearby, where, not every apartment had warm water available. My respect for these parents was immeasurable and I was amazed by their hard work in the fields, their resilience, and their desire to have their kids get a quality education.

That farm laborers are only now getting recognition as "essential workers," due to the pandemic, is long overdue! They have historically been ignored, sometimes demeaned, and always taken for granted by the general public. It does my heart good to see them finally get the recognition and respect for the vital work that they so arduously perform.

We had full classes in September, but the migratory families went back to Mexico or Texas to work on their homes and visit relatives during the school's Christmas vacation period and, often, even longer. Our staff looked forward to our classes returning to normal size and to witness the physical growth of the kids during the time they had been gone.

Most hadn't attended school while on hiatus, unfortunately, and this inhibited the improvement of their language development, Math, and social skills. On occasion, some families remained in Texas until the end of their respective school years. These students were, generally, not promoted into the next grade level, and, if they did return to Arizona in subsequent years, resulted in some not graduating from 8th grade until they were 15 or 16 years old.

Even in my first year as a teacher, it seemed that re-teaching the material to those returning from their winter hiatus seemed to be a terrible waste of time for those who didn't migrate. That was the impetus for the peer-teaching plan that was developed. The bi-lingual ability of most of our students was a blessing to our teaching staff and we celebrated this talent while really involving all the students in their own education.

In addition to the kids arriving to school in clean clothes, the parents took great pride in providing for their children's education and benefit whenever possible. This included: giving their children money to attend the annual county fair in October, exposing the students to exhibits, other agri-business careers, and to a large city; attending a week-long 6th grade Science Camp in the spring; participating in the "Roadrunner" marching band; playing sports; and, providing the very best clothing they could afford for 8th grade graduation ceremonies, up to and including formal gowns for the girls and tuxedos for the boys! The parents were very proud to witness their children graduating from 8th grade, as the vast majority of them had only attended school through the 6th grade in their native Mexico.

Even as hard as these parents were working out in the fields, they always attended parent conferences, school plays, night basketball games, band performances, fund-raising events, and community-wide dinners to support their kids and support those of us working in the school.

I would be derelict in my duty if I didn't recognize the several teachers and classified employees at this rural school who paid for private instrumental lessons for those students who possessed the talent and a drive to perform, but whose parents couldn't afford the extra cost of individual lessons. As a result of their generous contributions, our "Roadrunner" marching band received awards from nearby community parades and exemplary reviews in countywide competitions.

Additionally, I am grateful to our school board, who approved of the purchase of team uniforms for the various sports I coached, purchased basketball goals for the inside of our small cafeteria and a quality baseball backstop for our field, supported our school's attendance at the annual 6th grade Science Camp, supported the development of exploratory classes at the middle school level, and approved the needed Sex Education and Career Awareness classes I taught to the 7th and 8th graders, respectfully.

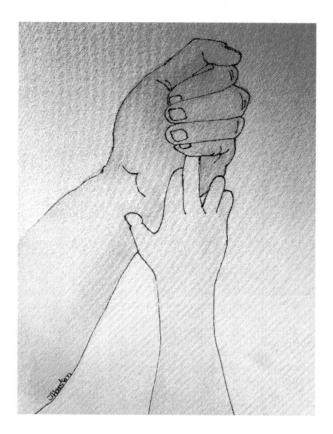

Chapter 8

Other Students

"Riff-Raff"

This was, of course, Julio's moniker for a set of Anglo twin brothers, whose father was a foreman at one of the ranches. They arrived at school in dirty and wrinkled clothing most days, only to get them even dirtier by day's end.

They also had a penchant for leaving crumpled up pictures of nude women around the room at the end of the school day, further justifying their nickname. Surmising that they had stumbled upon their father's treasure trove of girlie magazines, I just picked up after them whenever they deposited their discoveries around the room.

As these particular parents never attended regular school events or parent conferences, I never shared this behavior with them. They did attend the boys' graduation, however, but that was neither the time nor the place to have such a discussion about the behavior exhibited by their sons.

While not the best of students, either, the brothers have lived productive lives working on various ranches and farms throughout southern Arizona.

Juan

Juan was a handsome and bright young man who didn't particularly like me, as I had high expectations for him. He would give me the bare minimum of work (another example of karma), but did actively participate in classroom discussions. His participation was sometimes not appreciated by the other students, however, as Juan used these occasions to highlight his intelligence. "Smarty pants," of course, was an easily determined moniker from Julio.

One day, after coming in from lunch recess and yard duty, I noticed Juan within a small group of students directly behind me as I unlocked the door to the classroom. In the presence of other students, he was 'flipping the bird' at me, never expecting nor realizing that I could see his reflection in the door window I was facing. Without turning around, I grabbed the offending finger and told Juan that if I ever saw that again I would break it! To the delight of the other students around him, Juan was extremely embarrassed and quietly sulked for the rest of that week.

Juan went on to have a successful career in business and married life. I did get the opportunity to talk with him briefly at a local theater just a few years ago. He recognized me by my, I guess, distinctive gait, even 35 years after I taught him. He proudly introduced his two sons to my wife and me. After a brief conversation, I am certain, though, as my wife and I walked to our movie, he probably flipped me off again!

Antonio

While at this first school, I heard from the local high school Counselors that not many of our 8th grade graduates actually graduated from high school. In addition to their migratory family life, the next major reason seemed to be pregnancy-related.

I informed the School Board of these findings and also that the County Superintendent of Schools Office was sponsoring a one-day conference on teaching about venereal diseases. I offered to attend this conference and to teach this class, in hopes of reducing the number of dropouts of both male and female students from high school. I am pleased to say, that in the four years after starting this class, only one girl dropped out of high school due to pregnancy-related issues.

While some of the students were cognizant of the "birds and the bees" from, no doubt, living in close quarters with family members, almost all were deficient in knowledge about human growth and development, various sex acts, and venereal diseases one could contract.

Antonio was another handsome young man, very intelligent, almost six feet tall as a 7th grader, and had a full head of curly, black hair. He played on the basketball team (the "pro") I coached and was envied by the boys and dreamt of by the girls.

During one discussion about growth and development of the human sex organs, one of the students asked the average size of the penis during an erection. I answered that the average penis was between five to six inches long during an erection, when Antonio blurted out that his was "twelve inches!" After the classroom came back to order, and without asking Antonio anything else and to hide my own embarrassment about the outburst, I simply stated that, if that was true, he could be a movie star of sorts. Groans followed, giving evidence that most students did know something about porn, but it did take the spotlight off of Antonio and allowed the discussion to return to more appropriate discussions. I am positive that, during lunch recess, the more naïve students asked the more aware students about the movies I had referred to earlier.

It was Antonio who asked about oral sex, as well. I might add that this was the one topic with which the school board had expressed concern. I explained to the board that the topics of sex and venereal diseases required honesty and openness and that I would answer the questions in that manner if the topic came up. This pleased the school board, but questions about oral sex came up every single year!

I explained how this was performed, to the delight of a few and a shock to most. In order to save myself some embarrassment about this discussion, I usually ended the discussion about how I hoped we weren't having hot dogs or tacos in the cafeteria that day. This usually brought about more groans and laughter, and eased the uncomfortable feelings all of us were having.

In the four years I taught the venereal disease lessons, only one class was hesitant to ask their questions aloud, opting instead to write their questions down. As I had been discussing this topic in terms of "getting" and "giving" the diseases, I guess I shouldn't have been surprised when Anna (Yes, I could tell everyone's writing style.) wrote, "If you give a disease to someone else, do you still have it?" That was an OMG moment I still haven't forgotten, and I was immediately concerned and worried that former students might also have had that same misconception. Still somewhat reeling from that realization, my only response was that the "diseases are not like Christmas presents that you can just wrap up and give away. You still have the disease."

I never got any negative feedback from the other teachers, the school administrator, parents, or the school board about the hot dog/tacos comment or the discussion about the average length of a penis, as they were probably just happy that they didn't have to teach the subject!

Lydia and her brothers

Lydia arrived in my classroom as a shy and reserved young lady, when I was the 6th grade homeroom teacher my first four years. As her father was a ranch foreman, Lydia was one who tutored the more migratory students. Her intelligence was superior to most of the students I had taught during my early years and her parents attended every parent conference and Lydia's other activities.

It was during one of these conferences when I mentioned to her parents that Lydia had college potential. While somewhat surprised, but definitely proud of Lydia by this comment, they encouraged Lydia through her high school years, always reminding her of that goal.

During her 7th and 8th grade years, Lydia came out of her shell, was a Student Body Officer, and a cheerleader. As further proof of this transformation, Lydia's nickname at high school was "Miss Roadrunner" by both her peers and teachers. Lydia and her younger brothers, that I also had the pleasure of teaching, all attended college and are quite successful in their chosen careers.

I had the distinct pleasure of meeting Lydia a few years later, on the steps of the Registration Building at the college we both attended while I was getting an advanced degree. She had just completed her registration for summer classes and I was registering for classes towards my counseling credential. Lydia graduated from college and she remains an active and respected leader in her chosen field. She and her husband have attended the bi-annual reunions of staff and students from that rural elementary school when their schedules have allowed.

Her brothers were also gifted students and fine athletes. They went on to play high school and college baseball, and two of the three went on to graduate from college.

All lead successful lives. One is currently a high school Vice-Principal and one is retired after a full career as a Probation Officer.

I am able to stay in contact with each of them through social media and attendance at our bi-annual reunions. Antonio, the oldest of the brothers, recently visited me while I recovered from chemo treatments.

Chapter 9

More 'Here and Now' examples

The Drive-In

Many summer nights other Jr. High neighbors and I would walk down to the local drive-in theater (younger readers will have to ask their parents or grandparents about this) to watch movies for free. I had loosened a couple of boards from the back wall, for easy access to the movies, and we usually had money for candy, popcorn, and sodas. We sat next to one of the speakers so we could follow the conversation and plot of the movie.

Once again illustrating the 'here and now' thinking, rather than that of possible consequences, I tossed some pebbles back over the fence as we left the drive-in one night. Several high school boys didn't take fondly to their cars getting pelted, found our access point, began to chase us, and beat up my friends they caught.

My years of running from my older brother, evidently, gave me the speed and experience not to get caught. As the others wondered why they were "jumped," I feigned innocence as to any possible clue. The kind of attention I would have received from them was not the acceptance I desired!

The Seminary

While I attended the seminary, one incident in particular stands out. How this was planned or who initiated it remains a mystery to me at this time, but I went along willingly. (And if the reader believes that by now, I have some resort property in Alaska I'd like to sell you!) The seminary abutted up against the property of a Catholic high school, and we were able to use their athletic facilities after our school day. This included the gym, baseball fields, and pool.

The showers in the seminary's dorm consisted of two sets of seven or eight showers on either side of the middle entrance to them. Each shower was enclosed by metal sides, about five feet in height and with about a foot of clearance from the floor.

After swimming at the nearby pool one afternoon, two of my classmates and I decided to shower early, beating the rush of the others who would also shower before the evening meal. One of us suggested that it might be fun to slide down the floor, under the walls of the showers, on our bellies. We turned on all the showers, to get the floor moist and to enhance the sliding experience, and proceeded to play. Since clothing seemed to inhibit the sliding experience, off came our swim suits, as well.

Evidently, we were not quiet during this shenanigan, and were overheard by the priest who supervised the dorm. You can imagine his dismay at discovering three stark naked, wannabe priests, in this bizarre attempt to have some fun!

The three of us were ordered to get dressed and to report to his office after dinner. The rest of the dorm students were left wondering why the three of us were kneeling, just outside the priest's office, as they were preparing for the evening study hall. As we couldn't stop giggling over our experience every time we looked at one another, we were soon separated to complete our two-hour penances.

"Geez, Russell!" was the most often heard exclamation by our classmates as we prepped for bed that evening.

Nathaniel

Nathaniel was an 8th grader when I first met him and, again, one of the shortest boys in his class. He was always trying to get attention from the girls in his classes, but was never too successful. Some of these girls took to sunning themselves, in warm weather, during lunch. They lounged outside in an area between the cafeteria and the locker rooms.

Nathaniel confiscated a bottle of baby lotion from one of the girls, used then as a sun attractant, and proceeded to spray his initials, in letters about 4 feet tall, on the front of the locker room. As the locker room was a concrete building, however, Nathaniel's initials were only partially absorbed into the concrete and are still visible today, almost 20 years later! Yes, Nathaniel was the only boy in the entire school with the initials, "NT," and was easily identified and punished.

Nathaniel is leading a productive and successful life, and still resides in the community.

Troy

Troy was a small 7th grader, at another school entirely. He did try, however, the same kind of a stunt as Nathaniel. Troy and another male student in his class, decided to paint their initials in large, black letters on one of the walls behind the stage curtain. Instead of just painting his initials, however, Troy chose to put his first name and last initial. Again, the 'here and now' thinking came back to bite Troy, as he was the only Troy on campus with that same last name initial! I believe it took Troy and his co-conspirator 3-4 coats of paint to completely cover their attempt at graffiti. This was, of course, in addition to the 3-day suspension from school and all the projects his mother could find for him to complete around their house and the homes of their neighbors!

Troy has led a very successful adult life, is an exemplary father of two kids, maintains a bevy of pets for his children and their 4-H and FFA projects, and remains actively involved within the community and with his extended family.

Ezekiel

"Zeke" had earned his reputation as a rowdy student during his 6th and 7th grades and was an 8th grade student upon my initial meeting. That I had heard about Zeke while prepping for my first assignment as Principal, spoke volumes about him.

The perusal of his disciplinarian record illustrated that Zeke's most often rules violations, at a plethora of schools he had attended, involved making unnecessary remarks in the middle of classroom discussions, and defiance of his teachers and general school rules. While a tall and natural born leader, he spent more time trying to gain acceptance from his new peers than at studying. Yes, this was yet another example of karma that my own earlier attempts of gaining acceptance had prepared me for!

Our multipurpose room had an indoor stage that was utilized for band concerts, award ceremonies, an occasional community forum, and meetings with parents prior to the parent conferences. It also served as the school cafeteria and a gathering center for some students upon arriving at school. One of the rules at school was that no hats were to be worn inside any of the classrooms or any other building on campus.

I always stationed myself at the front of the school, so I could welcome the students and let them know that I was on campus if they needed to talk. It was no different this first day on the job in this new position, before going into the multipurpose room to meet and greet any students who mingled there before the first bell.

Sitting on the front of the stage was none other than Zeke, with his entourage of followers of both male and female 8th graders. Zeke, of course, was adorned in his baseball cap, as he felt his need to show his distain for that rule.

'No time like the present' was my initial thought and I walked up immediately to Zeke and his cohorts.

"Would you like to discuss your hat in front of your friends or should we have a private conversation?" I asked Zeke.

Zeke agreed to the private conversation, at which time I informed him that I would allow him to keep his cap this one time only, if he removed it from his head. Any other violations of the hat rule for the rest of the year would result in the confiscation of his hat for the rest of that week and the need for his mother to pick it up from my office.

Before returning to his friends, with his hat in his hand, I encouraged Zeke to visit me in my office if he ever had any questions or concerns I could assist him with. Pleasantly surprised, Zeke did request private conversations with me throughout the year. He informed me in one of our first meetings that he and his two siblings resided with his mother, as his father was out of the family picture for a variety of reasons.

Zeke also explained the rationale for the frequent moves he and his family made during his elementary school years. While valiantly attempting to keep her family together, Zeke's mother was undereducated, and the frequent loss of employment often meant moving to another community for work. She had finally found steady employment upon moving into our small town, allowing Zeke and his siblings some semblance of normalcy in his middle school years.

Zeke was fearful that he would follow in his father's footsteps, however, and envisioned no way to avoid this. Offering Zeke several alternatives to this behavior, the acceptance by his peers was still critical to him, and my attempts at personal, educational, and vocational counseling seemed almost futile.

While graduating from 8th grade with only minor disciplinary issues, and despite my best counseling, Zeke continued to occasionally challenge his teachers in high school. He was valiantly trying in his freshman year of high school to find outlets from his personal demons, however; speaking often with the high school counseling staff, searching for positive adult role models, and joining a church youth group, for example.

Zeke invited me to attend the Christmas Concert his church youth group supported and even introduced me to the congregation, as someone he admired and was blessed to have in his life. I lost contact with Zeke after his freshman year but was informed that his provocations in high school classes, and his never-ending battle over his personal demons, did eventually warrant his referral to the local continuation school.

A few years later, however, after attending a sports game with the "three amigos" and over a dinner meal and discussion of our lives, I was tapped on my shoulder by one of the wait staff.

"Are you my old school Principal?" Zeke asked.

I sat momentarily in stunned silence, initially not recognizing the adult version of Zeke. In our brief conversation, Zeke explained to me that he had continued his errant ways through and beyond high school, but was now successfully addressing all the issues that had bothered him previously.

It had turned out that this restaurant, suggested to us by Andy, who was now a probation officer, was one aspect of Zeke's counseling program. In addition to the counseling he was still receiving, this program also provided career opportunities in such fields as restaurant occupations and semi-truck driving.

Zeke has gone on to be a successful semi-truck driver and continues to successfully address and control his personal concerns.

Marco

Marco arrived at our school mid-way through his 7th grade year and was escorted to school by his father and his Probation Officer. As his cumulative file was not yet in our possession, the parties informed me that Marco had spent most of his life living with his mother and in transit from city to city and, therefore, from school to school. During our initial conversation, Marco was not hesitant to express his utter disregard for school and for his prior incarcerations in local juvenile halls.

Despite our introductory counseling session and his teachers' attempts to assign positive students as models and guides, Marco was suspended the very next morning, for putting super glue in the lock of his "homeroom" door. It seems that Marco had found two like-minded students, the first day during lunch recess, and they enjoyed learning of this new prank.

While at first denying any knowledge of the incident, security footage from the cameras we had installed the summer before was enough evidence for the parents of his two abettors and Marco's father and his Probation Officer; each, wholeheartedly agreeing with the fairness of the discipline administered. Again, the 'here and now,' the need for acceptance, and Marco's personal distain for school, far outweighed the positive change in his living arrangements and any concern for consequences, even another stay in Juvenile Hall.

The Probation Officer's reaction was swift and decisive, leading to an extensive stay in Juvenile Hall and eventual foster care for Marco. Marco's life, according to his father, continued in a downward spiral and resulted in criminal behavior and incarcerations.

Chapter 10

Familial Teachers

My Parents

While my father was the chief disciplinarian in the family, quick to administer corporal punishment for my many transgressions, my mother could usually get the results she wanted with a stern look and a raised eyebrow. My two brothers, my sister, and I were raised in a strict Catholic and military family. Children "were to be seen and not heard" and if our noise interrupted adult conversation or activities, punishment and/or a stern lecture was to follow. "Yes, sir" and "Yes, ma'am," along with "Please" and "Thank you," were the expected norms.

I believe to this day, that this upbringing created the reserved and observant student and adult I was to become. My juvenile pranks and acceptance-getting misbehaviors were probably, also, initiated by this same upbringing, as there was a need to break away from the strictness, in and out of school, and initiate some fun activities. Being the middle, and the shortest, of the three brothers could also have been factors in the need to be noticed and gain acceptance on my own terms. The fact that we were transferred from Illinois, to Texas, and to Arizona, from 3rd-5th grades, also sparked the need for quick acceptance by my peers. Additionally, our family changed residential neighborhoods during my 5th, 6th and 7th grade years and I yearned to be accepted by new neighbors.

Upon entering the 7th grade, my parents were able to purchase their first home, and we moved into, yet, another new neighborhood. This house was the first that our parents were able to purchase, after years of living in base housing or renting. Justifiably proud of this achievement, they took great care in selecting a corner lot, in the selection of interior and exterior paint colors our mother wanted, and in the installation the grass and shrubs. As it was my primary responsibility to mow and edge the lawn, in our more than 50 years of marriage, my wife and I have yet to live on another corner lot, due to the expanse of the side yard I had to maintain!

My siblings and I shared dinner duties; with one setting and clearing the table, one washing dishes, and one drying them. As there were four of us, each received one week off from our "KP" (Kitchen Patrol) duties. It was on one of these occasions that I decided to trip my younger brother as he carried a full armload of dishes to the sink, right in front of our parents. Even the 'here and now' mindset didn't make any sense whatsoever in this event and my punishment was immediate and painful!

We each made our own beds, picked up our clothes daily, and learned to vacuum and mop; as to somewhat relieve mom from her other in-house and career obligations.

Dad's hastiness in administering discipline was not without some mistakes, however. As evidence, after my older brother overheard my father explain to me at what level he wanted the lawn to be mowed, my brother secretly reset the mower lower. I ended up tearing up part of the fresh lawn but, luckily, stopped before scalping it entirely. Dad was extremely disappointed in me, nonetheless, and I was once again, but undeservedly so in this incident, on the receiving end of his corporal punishment.

Mom's form of punishment did not usually involve the same physical pain as our father's. I distinctly remember my punishment for slamming a door one day was to quietly open and close the door twenty times before I was allowed to continue my play. We both ended up in laughter before

I had completed my task, but her form of punishment ended the door-slamming problem once and for all.

I only saw our mother use violence to resolve a problem once. This, once again, involved my older brother. While lagging behind in height all the way through my junior year of high school, I did grow to be 5'8" the summer between my junior and senior years, and only about an inch shorter than him.

During a rare pick-up game of basketball, he became quite pushy whenever he had the ball. Despite my protests he continued this tactic, as I grew angrier and angrier. When he did miss a shot that went up on the roof, I turned around and slammed the ball into his face. The war was on!

For a change, however, I held my own and got in a few good punches. After a short while, he grabbed me, threw me to the ground, and jumped on top.

From the kitchen window, mom saw us fighting and brought a broom with her to break us up. At the moment she arrived, my brother was still on top of me and I had him in headlock. Rather violently, she started hitting my brother in the back with the broom, all the while exclaiming, "Let him up!"

While this was going on, I was slamming his face into the pavement gleefully saying, "Yeah, let me up! Let me up!" Bloodied from his nose and eyebrow, he went to clean up but never challenged me again to a fight.

In addition to being the primary disciplinarian, our father also was our first baseball coach and taught my brothers and me the arts of fielding and pitching. Dad was a gifted softball player, himself, playing catcher for his Air Force base team, and bringing with him a knowledge base for his coaching.

In addition to the personal attention I received from his coaching, I remember most fondly attending our high school's annual Sports Awards Banquet and the shoulder rub from his massive hands as we advanced in the potluck line. Although never comfortable to actually verbalize it, this was his manner of illustrating his pride in me.

His baseball mentorship was successfully utilized up to my first year at the state college I attended. It was there I learned that I would never be able to hit a first-rate breaking ball and gave any dream of being a professional baseball player.

Upon his retirement from the Air Force, dad shared with me his first retirement check. After 22 years of service, it was only $300! Dad explained that if he had attended OCS, (Officer Candidate School) which he was encouraged to do by several supervising officers, his check would have had "an extra zero at the end."

Like my father, I ignored the suggestion from the first two Principals I worked under, that I seek an Administrative Credential. I did begin taking classes in Counseling and Administration when the third Principal, whom I admired greatly, also made the same suggestion. I vividly remembered seeing my father's first retirement check, and hearing his regrets about not going to OCS. Getting my advanced credentials allowed me to retire at age 60, financially secure, and without any regrets whatsoever.

Like Sister Agnes before him, this third Principal truly enjoyed working with students! He changed our school through his daily example of a positive work ethic and creating a culture in which the staff worked with him instead of for him.

Dad also introduced me to fishing and golf, which I enjoy and participate in to this day.

Mom, however, was the rock and the foundation of our family. She was both mother and father when dad was deployed or finding housing in advance of our next move. Working from 7AM to 3PM at the hospital, she was able to attend most of the afterschool baseball games and provided quiet guidance throughout our lives.

She was also true to her Catholic faith until her dying day and it was due to her role modeling that dad converted to the Catholic faith. She provided the support, teamwork, and encouragement expected of wives back then and insisted that we would all be baptized Catholic, attend parochial schools, and participate in the other rites of the church. Both parents attended the basketball and football games, as they were usually contested in the evenings.

Mother never found out about my most serious juvenile offenses as dad had forbidden any mention of them to her. He simply told all of us that such knowledge would "probably kill her." Luckily, even my older brother adhered to this dire warning.

Mom had an abiding faith in God and the teachings of the Catholic Church. It should be noted that Catholics were not supposed to use any form of birth control, then, and was considered a mortal sin. She actually gave birth to six boys, but three died shortly after birth, due to a rare blood factor issue. It was only their deep, abiding faith in God and in each other that explains how my parents went on after those devastating events.

So serious and dedicated she was about her faith, she even cried upon the realization that I occasionally missed Sunday Mass while I attended college. While still not attending weekly, I did make sure I shaved before visiting again on weekends!

She believed in the sanctity of marriage and of Good Friday. When I was 15, she shared with me that all in her family had died on Fridays, except her divorced sister. Divorce was also a mortal sin according to the Catholic faith and mom intimated that her sister's divorce angered God and she, therefore, died on a different day of the week.

At 23, when I was in my second year of teaching, mom died after a long, arduous battle with cancer. She was down to about 75 pounds and had been in a coma for three weeks before I remembered our conversation about the importance of Fridays. As none of my siblings had heard of this personal story, I went alone to be with my father at her bedside late Thursday night. Knowing that hearing was the last sense remaining to the dying, at midnight I whispered, "Hi, Mom, this is Russell. It is now Friday and it's okay to let go." She passed ten minutes later.

The doctors explained that they were amazed that she hadn't died right after going into the coma, as she was so very weak. I knew the explanation and kept it to myself. I still regret that I didn't remember the conversation of my youth much sooner.

My Wife

As stated earlier, I met my future wife at a downtown dance. Mandy was a senior in high school and I was a freshman in college. We dated for a couple of months before I offered her my high school ring and asked her to "go steady." She was the first girl I dated that refused to go steady when I asked her, and, having hurt feelings (hypersensitivity), I didn't intend to ever see her or ask her out again. As fate would have it though, I saw her two months later at another dance in a nearby community and we began dating again. We dated for two years before we married.

The intervening two years were not without trials and tribulations for her, as I was still very immature and drinking on most weekends. When my car was impounded, after an unsuccessful drinking event and after being driven to town cuffed and in the back of a sheriff's car, she and her cousin picked me up and drove me home. Luckily for me, the sheriff's officer charged me incorrectly, I was found not guilty, and this indiscretion never gave me a record. More importantly, my mother never heard of this event, either.

On another occasion, she and I ended up walking about 5 miles to her home when my car broke down. My younger brother came to the rescue that evening and my father and I retrieved my car the next morning. Much to her on-going chagrin all these years, I still have little to no mechanical ability.

In spite of these shortcomings, Mandy saw more in me than I saw in myself. Her faith that I would eventually mature and be successful was rewarded after we married and I completed my undergraduate studies in 1970.

It was Mandy who showed me that there were other means of disciplining our own children, besides the heavy-handed manner in which I was raised.

While I was accustomed to moving from one place to another, because of the Air Force, Mandy was raised outside of town, actually lived on a street named after her family, and never moved from her home until we married.

She put down roots quickly wherever we moved, but was also very reluctant to move for my career advancements or new assignments. As it took time to sell our home in each community, she and our children remained in the "old place" before moving to be with me. While I was commuting home on weekends until she and the kids could be with me, she was both father and mother for these intervals, just as my mother had been after my father was deployed or transferred from base to base.

Mandy postponed her plans to be a Physical Therapist upon the birth of our children, to remain at home with them until they both started school. The distance to a college with this program, the need to supplement my salary, and the ever-changing prerequisites for Physical Therapy, however, caused her to permanently surrender her plans. That she did this illustrates her commitment to our family and established the values with which our children adhere to, and believe in, to this very day.

Mandy was a secretary while I completed my undergraduate degree, but became a classroom aide when our own children started in school. She remained an aide upon every move we made, earning praise for her teaching, her secretarial skills, and the manner in which she monitored and mentored her assigned students.

It is said that most men marry up. In my case, that is definitely true and I give thanks daily for her loving support and, when needed, guidance. I remain truly blessed to have her in my life.

My Younger Brother

My younger brother, Keith, is three years younger than me, and 5 years younger than our older brother. Not only did we share a bedroom with our older brother, we also shared our dislike for him as we both were on the receiving end of his teasing and abuse.

Keith and I enjoyed shooting baskets, throwing darts, playing tackle football, or playing catch, but we purposefully didn't include our older brother. Because of my small stature, Keith and I were evenly matched in our youth despite the age differential. The only time an injury occurred was the day I tackled him on the goal line, which was the sidewalk! The resultant broken collarbone sidelined him for about a month and our playtime was limited to indoor activities and no-contact play outdoors.

Despite the broken collarbone and my tripping him with his arms full of dishes, we continued to enjoy each other's company and spent many afternoons and evenings playing, including a game we called "kick back." It was contested out in the street in front of the house, each trying to kick a football over the other's head until moving him back to the next corner.

As he grew, however, his prowess at kicking that ball became much greater than mine and I took to throwing the football to even give myself a chance against his mighty left foot. I believe to this day that throwing that ball gave me the arm strength to pitch successfully through high school. He went on to be the starting tight end and punter for our high school's football team, at the local community college, and for a time, at the university level.

He is capable of adapting to any situation. He changed his faith to the Mormon Church upon his marriage. He successfully sold farm equipment and clothing, beginning without an iota of knowledge about either. Later, he successfully sold, installed, and maintained home alarm systems, again, without an initial base of knowledge.

He has since retired and he and his wife moved to Hawaii, learning the customs and local lingo quickly. It was upon our first visit to their home when he introduced me to their neighbors and friends as his "Bruddah!"

Keith was occasionally a co-conspirator in getting even with our older brother for his bullying. My older brother and I shared a double bed through the fifth grade, but Keith had his own, because he had a tendency to thrash around at night.

We often jumped from one bed to the other, using a chair in between the beds as a medial step. We also threw darts at the foot of the other as he stepped on the chair! While Keith and I would get a dart in our foot on occasion, I took this opportunity to throw at our older brother's legs. Anywhere from ankle to knee was my target and his injuries reflected my good aim.

It was Keith who loaned me money, and drove me around collecting soda bottles and the wooden containers, to earn enough money to get my car out of the impound garage.

When Mandy and I moved back to our hometown after college, it was Keith who volunteered whenever he could to assist in the moving process and in preparing our new yard.

He has been an inspiration through his faith, his work ethic, his commitment to his family, and through his guidance. I am a much better person with him in my life.

Chapter 11

Formal Educators

My first recollection of a teacher that I respected actually occurred when I was in summer school after the second grade. While not remembering his name, I appreciated that he sat on the front of his desk and actually talked to us instead of talking at us. I remembered that example as I began teaching, aping his position on the front of my desk often, conversing with my classes, and teaching to and with them instead of just lecturing at them. In truth, I learned as much, or more, from them as they learned from me.

Coach Avila

Coach Avila was at the parochial school when we arrived in southern Arizona, teaching Physical Education/Health classes at both the elementary and secondary levels, and coaching the varsity basketball and baseball teams for the high school.

While also short in stature, I always marveled at his ability to remain in excellent physical shape "for a man his age." Boxing, it appeared upon closer inspection of his slightly misshapen nose, seemed to have formed the core of his athletic endeavors in his youth.

Truth be told, the athletic teams I played on improved minimally under his tutelage, but I will always appreciate his willingness to devote his time and energy to the sports and the manner in which he related to each individual student/athlete. As I wasn't 5' tall until mid-way through the baseball season of my Jr. year, I was gratified he saw the pitching prowess I possessed and allowed me to flourish those last two years in high school. His example as a teacher and coach was the reason I chose to major in Physical Education and become a coach. While I may have been a better coach, I still strive to match his standards in teaching and in humanity.

I also observed the principled and respectful manner in which he related to the religious around campus. Coach's defense of them even included once confronting and challenging a parent who had overstepped the bounds in his treatment of our new Principal, Sister Agnes!

Sister Agnes

After Sister Margaret left our Catholic school, she was replaced my junior year of high school by Sister Agnes. What a revelation! I witnessed first hand how one person could positively alter the culture of a school, through her example to other teachers and students. Under her leadership, the nuns became kinder and the former negative disciplinary practices ceased.

Sister Agnes actually enjoyed students! She attended basketball and baseball games, initiated a fashion show to support the educational extras, taught English classes and, again, talked with her students instead of just at them. She publicly expressed her pride in her teaching staff, once taking the microphone before our Christmas performance of the Glee Club and extolling the talent and dedication of our teacher, Sister Christine. While she was not aware, I observed and learned from her, consequently attending as many student activities as I could and, hopefully, extending adequate praises to the staff members I had the pleasure of working with throughout my administrative tenure.

Her disciplinary methods were mature and very much appreciated, whether a look of disapproval or a terse reminder about school rules. "Mr.

Morrow, do you need to chew your gum so blatantly?" This comment not only improved my vocabulary but also eliminated that particular practice.

Another incident that she handled with aplomb, and without demeaning the student, was when she noticed one male student with a mouthful of chew during lunch recess. She pleasantly conversed with this student until she noticed him swallow his rules violation. He never chewed tobacco at school again, as he remembered this incident and his resultant rushed visit to the toilet in the boys' restroom.

Southern Arizona Administrators

As stated earlier, one can learn from negative examples as well as from positive ones. The first two administrators at the small country school where I was employed are primary examples. Both were bullies and their everyday interactions with staff made it evident that we worked for them instead of with them.

The first, Mr. McIntyre, had been the Principal/Superintendent for several years before I was hired in 1970. He ruled with an iron fist and staff meetings were directive in nature, rather then collegial. That this time period was the beginning of Collective Bargaining for school employees only made him angrier, as he perceived it as an infringement on his ability to rule.

Like most bullies, he took the new system as a personal affront and reacted predictably. As an example, he tied positive teacher evaluations for Mr. Bennett with Mr. Bennett's reports back to him of our association meetings. "Quid pro quo" is a favorite tool of all bullies, whether still of school age or later in adult life. Additionally, he somehow convinced the school board that the installation of a time clock in the office was necessary, when in actuality, he was the only one ever late for work! Since I was so mechanically retarded, though, my time card was unreadable, as I kept double-clicking my card into the machine. Who knew I was so nervous and that clumsy!

His dictatorial manner led to pickets at our school board meetings, and the staff of 12 teachers from this small rural school had support from about 60 school union members from throughout the county. The installation of the time clock was ridiculed in newspaper editorials from throughout the county. Mr. McIntyre's anger grew to the point that contract negotiations for salary and benefits came to a complete halt.

As I was now President of the local teachers' association, he and I agreed to self-eliminate from the negotiations, opting for others to represent our respective views. A former board member volunteered to represent the district and he and the regional union representative came to a quick resolution, which the board approved.

As is the case with most bullies, Mr. McIntyre placed the blame for the impasse and the negative press about the time clock at my feet and began to degrade me to all the other administrators in the county. So much so, that the director of the regional science camp was told by his boss, the

County Superintendent of Schools, that he couldn't hire me, as I was a "troublemaker."

The second administrator, Mr. Munoz, selected by the school board to eventually replace Mr. McIntyre, was also out of touch with the new reality of collective bargaining and attempted to dictate all aspects of the various jobs within the school, whether certificated or classified. Intimidation was his first ploy, adorning his office walls with copies of his supposed credentials, and threatening to move teachers to grade levels that they were unfamiliar with and unprepared for. His tactics were easily described in full to the school board and he was quickly dismissed.

Neither of these administrators ever exhibited any positive regard for students: neither made an attempt to watch the students participate in any sports, band, nor academic activity; neither welcomed the students and staff to school each morning; and, neither recognized the good that students or staff achieved.

Both of these adult bullies were eventually forced to vacate their careers; Mr. McIntyre for theft from the district and Mr. Munoz for his general negative demeanor and his continued false and illegal claims regarding his educational credentials.

Northern Arizona Administrators

After my 5-year stint as a Vocational Counselor, I was hired to be a Counselor in an even more remote corner of northern Arizona; home to sagebrush, cacti, Indian reservations, a state prison, and a cast of characters one will never forget.

As a high school Counselor for one year, I was able to work with, observe, and learn from three administrators, as this particular campus population was large enough to warrant having two Vice-Principals in addition to the Principal. Each was blessed with their individual styles and unique methods of dealing with staff and students. I will always be grateful for the manner in which they treated and mentored me. They explained their decisions and gave of their advice freely and without judgment, taking me into their confidence and under their collective wings, as they knew my time there would be limited.

Truly, my greatest learning experience was to follow when I was hired the very next year at the local middle school, as Vice-Principal. For seven years, I had the pleasure of being mentored by one of the finest people I have ever had he pleasure of working with. Again, with instead of for!

Tom Boyd was Principal during my years as Vice-Principal. He welcomed me, introduced me to the staff and to the culture of the school, and mentored me during my entire tenure there.

Most of his quiet mentoring was through his steady and calm demeanor, whether dealing with community concerns, personnel issues, or in his dealings with the Superintendent's Office or School Board members. He was extremely elated, though, to dump the duty of receiving, counting, and stamping the new textbooks to me on my second day on the job!

Tom was a devout Christian, an involved parent and husband, and, at that time, a deacon in his church. He truly lived his lay life exhibiting, but not preaching, those religious tenets. He exemplified it in all his dealings with people, whether they worked inside or outside of the school system.

This was not always easy to do in a "prison town," where spouses and children often followed their imprisoned relatives into a new community close to the prison. Their fathers, of course, were not customarily good role models and this contributed to many of the discipline problems at school. Tom handled these issues with patience and grace, guiding me along the way.

The primary example of prisoners not growing beyond the 7th grade mentality occurred one day when a bus load of prisoners, on outside duty for good behavior, came to our school during Easter break. Their duties involved raking up leaves, pinecones and needles, and performing other general cleanup. After admiring one of our female employees, an inmate decided to throw a rake under her car, so she would have to bend over to retrieve it.

His pleasure was short-lived, as I notified the Sergeant on duty of this event and he immediately ordered the inmates back to the bus for the quick ride back to the prison.

Monitoring and guarding inmates remanded to medium or maximum-security prisons is not an easy task, either. The frustration correctional officers felt sometimes carried over to the schools, in the form of loud or obnoxious behavior in disciplinary meetings about their own children. Upon learning that a neighbor of mine was an administrator at the prison, however, their fits of temper were quelled and brought the decibel level of the discussions down to normal speaking tones.

Tom also had a tremendous sense of humor, which he displayed often on the playground with students, in staff meetings, or with the office staff. When I mentioned to him that the Principal at the high school had a habit of clipping his fingernails to signify the end of a meeting, it was Tom (honestly!) who thought of distributing the clippings from horse hooves around this principal's office while he was away.

Tom asked a community member for clippings from the hooves of his horses and those clippings "mysteriously" appeared in this principal's coffee cup, in the overhead lighting fixtures, inside his private restroom, inside desk drawers, and anywhere else we thought of. The principal found hoof clippings somewhere in his office for the rest of the school year!

Whether or not it changed his habit or not, we were both too afraid of ever asking. What fun we had, though!

Our male PE teacher had a habit of eating his lunch in his classroom, instead of in, what then was, a negative teachers' lounge environment. Tom and I convinced the students, during lunch playground supervision, to roll up a huge snowball and place it in front of this teacher's door. The snowball grew to about 6' in diameter and all of us enjoyed the teacher's futile and hilarious five minutes of attempts to egress from his classroom!

Simpatico! As those seven years passed, I began to appreciate that Tom and I had a bond that went back to both of us having been "immature 7th grade boys." Tom and I regaled each other about our youthful indiscretions, while attempting to keep our own families, our students, and our school staff unaware of these.

Returning South

As my father was ill, it was time to search for an administrative position closer to him and to where I grew up. Within an hour's drive from him, I was offered the position of Principal of a dynamic middle school campus, inheriting a tremendous staff of teachers and classified employees. Evaluation of the employees was simple, as the great majority of the staff was dedicated to enhancing the education of all of their students. The School Superintendent and School Board of Education must be thanked, as they had created a thorough hiring procedure that vetted out the less desirable applicants for administrative, teaching, or classified positions.

As the primary example of the quality staff that I worked with, I introduced the concept of the school applying for a "Distinguished Middle School" award from the Arizona State Department of Education. At a staff meeting, I listed the areas of criteria for this recognition that our staff was already successfully performing.

The only component that appeared to be missing, to achieve this well-deserved recognition, was the need for more student-counseling activities and I introduced a program I called, "All, for One." Every employee, certificated and classified, was encouraged to take one shy or isolate student under his or her wing. (Classified staff included secretaries, classroom aides, cooks, janitors, and the librarian.) Each participating staff member celebrated their student's birthday and good report cards, talked and listened to them whenever problems arose, suggested alternative responses to issues they faced, and generally encouraged their student's success.

At the introductory meeting regarding our future application, several teachers volunteered to respond to specific sections of the application. I, then, edited the application so as to appear to have been written with one voice. The school and staff was awarded the first "Distinguished Middle School" recognition in its history, after just one year of supporting the "All, for One" program, and continuing all that they already did on behalf of our students.

In the second year of this program, the staff evolved the program into, "All, for One-or Two!"

As stated earlier, I was blessed to work with such a dedicated staff and the school staff has justifiably earned this prestigious state award two additional times.

Chapter 12

Other Good Kids

Christopher was already a great student when he arrived in the 6th grade to our school. He grew to be very tall before graduating from the 8th grade three years later but, much to the chagrin of our coaches, Christopher was never interested in playing sports. What set Christopher apart from all the other students was his penchant for involving some of the student isolates in pick-up basketball games and other activities during lunch recess. I observed this often and actually designed the successful "All, for One." counseling program based on his behavior!

Christopher continues to reside in the same community, has a wonderful family, and is a Pastor at a local church. We occasionally have the opportunity, and privilege for me, to play golf together. While he tolerates my political views and opinions on social media, he is kind not to preach about some of my less than flattering language.

Several students from each of the schools I served have gone on to serve in the military. Some have even reached superior ranks and positions;

including becoming Navy Seals, pilots, and one who is now a ranking NCO of the entire Navy!

Others have joined the educational ranks, currently serving as aides, teachers, bus drivers, coaches, or in Administration. Numerous are leading productive lives in Agriculture, Politics, the Film Industry, Small Business, Medicine, Financial Planning, Engineering, and more.

Evan

I had the distinct pleasure of getting to know and work with Evan all three years he was at the middle school. As he was the child of one of the School Board members, he was an exemplary student, but reticent as a 6th grade student to express or bring attention to himself. He blossomed in his last two years, becoming a student leader on the Student Council. His personal, social, and educational growth continued through high school and college.

Evan returned from college and joined his father in the family farming business. He has encouraged his father to experiment with new crops and provided wise agricultural knowledge to the expanding business. Evan remains in the local area, is raising his own family, and has replaced his father as a member on the School Board.

Lessons of politeness remain with Evan, from the teachings of his parents. I have the pleasure of seeing and visiting with Evan on occasion. Asked now to just refer to me as "Russell," Evan refuses, stating, "I can't do that. You will always be Mr. Morrow to me."

Chapter 13

Bullies

Bullies are the very worst, bar none! The bullies are really cowards themselves, but make life at school miserable for all those around them, including teachers, custodial and other classified staff, administrators, and, worst of all, their targeted students. They are also, many times, one of the shorter boys in class but are backed up by some of the taller ones. They generally take the lead because the others are wise enough not to and this feeds their need for acceptance from his cowardly peers.

The fact that short-term and long-term negative effects may impact their targets receives not one iota of recognition at the time. In actuality, they continue to bully because of their own inferiority feelings. They feel miserable and want others to feel just as miserable, negative results not withstanding. A few do, thank goodness, attempt to make amends in the weeks, months, and years that follow.

In many cases the bullying is encouraged by, and copied from, adults in their lives. In rare cases, that adult might even be a teacher who was a bully herself/himself. Some of these teachers use "emotional blackmail" techniques in the classroom; providing positive feedback when appropriate but are verbally abusive when he or she doesn't get the desired academic or behavioral results. Unfortunately, this negative behavior is on display in the presence of the other students in class, embarrassing the victim and frightening the rest. Some, usually coaches, are physically and verbally abusive. Most of these suffer from "little man syndrome" and use their positions to belittle students and athletes.

In disciplining the bullies, I have often witnessed bullying tactics in existence within the home, as well. The most memorable, despicable, and heartbreaking case I encountered occurred upon suspending a bully and taking him home. Immediately upon opening the front door, the son was charged by his father. The father was about to hit his son, with his fists, before realizing that I was standing, within view, on the front porch.

While totally understanding the father's frustration upon seeing his son suspended again, it gave me insight into one reason the bully behaves in a like manner. I attempted to counsel this particular parent, but to no avail. (This occurred, I might add, before the "required reporting" standards for educators, medical staff, and others became law.) Tragically, the bullying by this young man continued throughout high school and beyond, and resulted in his death during another attempted bullying incident.

Bullying can also come from girls and their cliques. Whether from either sex, however, bullying is the predominant reason many adults do not remember their middle school years more fondly.

I have to admit to being grateful for my retirement before the technology that has resulted in cyber-bulling, as I have not had to be witness to the dire results, up to and including suicide, of some victims.

Roberto and Jaime

Brothers Roberto and Jaime arrived early in their 7th and 8th grade years, respectfully. It was apparent to me, within minutes, that Roberto was the hot- tempered one and Jaime, the older and calmer one. They were now living with a relative, in order to get them away from the gang influence of their native city.

As part of my introduction to them in the ways of their new school, I informed them that it was not necessary for them to challenge anyone, as gangs were not prevalent and no one on campus was a threat to them.

Roberto was back in my office directly after lunch recess, however, for fighting whom he believed was the tallest boy he could beat up. After this initial 3-day suspension, and other similar fighting incidents, Roberto finally accepted and believed the review I had given him that first day, having a much more productive 8th grade year.

Jaime had an excellent 8th grade year and high school, even while attempting to keep Roberto out of fights and out of trouble.

Roberto resorted back to his troublesome ways at high school, and Jaime to his attempts to save his younger brother. They attended a party in a rougher community, during their Jr. and Sr. years and Roberto got into an argument while there. In attempting to get Roberto out of the confrontation, however, Jaime was shot in the stomach. Luckily, he survived, and Roberto used this experience to seriously contemplate his bullying tactics and angered reactions to perceived insults.

Roberto has calmed down in adulthood and both are living productive lives.

Ian

I was quite familiar with Ian's residence as I took him home after each of his several suspensions from school, usually for bullying or fighting, and grew to know his father quite well.

As a runner most of my adult life, I ran regularly around the communities in which I worked. While changing routes almost daily to ward off boredom, I did occasionally run by the apartment where Ian lived. On one such occasion, I heard a projectile of some sort, whiz by my head. I looked up in time to see a gun barrel disappear from the side fence of Ian's apartment.

I knocked on Ian's door and talked with his father. Ian was immediately summoned and ordered to bring his pellet gun with him. Rather than have me describe this incident to the local police authorities, Ian's father agreed to destroy the weapon and immediately broke the gun over his knee.

I never had another disciplinary problem with Ian, nor do I know what he has become as an adult.

David

David moved into our community mid-way through his 7th grade year. He lived with his father, an ex-convict, in a singlewide, dilapidated trailer.

Within the first week of his attendance, David was given detention every day and, then, was suspended for three days on Friday, for fighting. Several more suspensions followed over the course of that first few months of attendance, due to his outright defiance of his teachers, bulling other students in his attempts to establish his place at the top of the pecking order, and sexual harassment of some of the female students.

Since there was no phone in the home, I took David home all too often. Upon one such occasion, utilizing prison mentality and vernacular, David's father threatened to have me killed! This was more out of frustration with his son than actual anger at me, and with some "reality therapy" counseling regarding my close relationship with the local police, David's father readily apologized for his threat. Though David received suspension punishments again, I wasn't the recipient of any further threats.

David didn't return for his 8th grade year, moving with his father, and I never heard from or about him, again.

Chapter 14

Initialed "Names"

Please, never, call your son by just his initials! These students generally consider themselves entitled, better than others, and above the rules. This attitude is present and on exhibition in the lower grades, through middle and high school, and, often, into adulthood.

These students are also some of the worst bullies on campus, as they are supported by others and are emboldened to make school miserable for others. The parents, generally, don't see and don't want to believe this at the primary levels.

While some parents refuse to believe that "my child" would be a bully, a few listened to the school's concerns and took pro-active measures in addressing the concerns. One parent, whom I respected very much, requested a parent conference for all of the parents of the clique his son identified with. From that discussion, this parent volunteered to help supervise the students during lunch recess. As he knew all the parents of this clique, this creative and much appreciated endeavor halted all the harassment on campus and any concern the other parents might have had that, as the Vice-Principal, I was picking on their students.

Many with initials went on to less than successful lives. More than one actually died in their early twenties, at the hands of someone bigger and more vicious. Two were killed drunk driving shortly after high school, several continued to abuse their own children and other family members, and many abused alcohol and drugs. Divorce was not an uncommon outcome for those that continued their egocentric "me first" attitude. Maturity, it seems, stopped at the 7th grade level.

Only two, that I recall, have lived productive and stable adult lives. One was the one whose father volunteered to supervise at lunch recess and one who only used the initials, "R.C," through the 4th grade.

M.O.I.

While his initials were actually MOI, his parents and friends referred to him simply as "Mo." He learned in 7th grade, of course, that the totality of his initials was French for "me," and he began to identify his books and binders with the capitol letters, "ME." His behavior went even further downhill after this revelation.

Egocentric to the max, "Mo" truly felt as if the world revolved around him and his wants. Younger siblings who later went through the same school, informed me of some of the abuses from him. "What's mine is mine, and what's yours is mine," infuriated not only his siblings but also many of his peers.

MO was in my office for discipline issues throughout his middle school years. Most of these events were related to stealing, sexual harassment, or bullying. Telephone calls, parent conferences, counseling, suspensions, and other disciplinary actions resulted only in short-lived improvements. Only through the threat of expulsion and the transfer to a Continuation School were the negative behaviors quelled, at both the middle and high school levels.

Unfortunately, his employment history has been replete with dismissals from work, due to drug or sexual abuse. His marriages were ruined due to his frequent affairs and his abusive parental disciplinary actions. To this day, his former wives and most of his children want nothing to do with him.

Chapter 15

Full-moon Fridays and Wind

Every school employee, at whatever level, is cognizant of the odd events and behaviors that full-moon Fridays and windy days bring. When combined with the hormonal ebb and flow at the middle school level, however, unexpected events and behavior seem in greater proportion than those at the primary or high school levels. This is probably the reason other educators wonder about the sanity of those of us who work with middle school students.

Even the best of students can and will occasionally be involved in bizarre events and behaviors, in the classroom or out on the playground, during these days. Full-moon Fridays and wind have no respect for the good and well-adjusted young teens, their parents, or their teachers! All parents should be alerted to and aware of this weirdness before their student hits puberty. They should also not be surprised to receive a call from a teacher, counselor, school nurse, or administrator on one of these days.

One such memorable event involved two 7th grade boys wrestling over a piece of bamboo, just after returning to the classroom from lunch recess. As one went to throw the shattered and splintered piece of bamboo into the garbage, the other grabbed it from behind to, once again, control the stick. The resultant injuries included bloodied slices to all five fingers of the "victor." I returned to class, bandages and band-aids in place, and still have one visible scar on that hand!

Windy days energize, excite, and distract students more so than any other, except full-moon Fridays. Getting and keeping students' attention and involvement is challenged to the utmost. Recesses bring more injuries, more bullying, and more disciplinary events than normal. "What on God's green earth were you thinking?" is not an uncommon refrain from teachers, administrators, and parents on these days.

On the positive side, this current pandemic has brought about a renewed respect for teachers and others who deal with students. Many parents, facing the distance-learning and home-school challenges, have utilized social media to vent their own frustrations and, also, their new-found respect and appreciation for classroom teachers and aides. Full-moon Fridays and windy days still occur and are, now, frustrating even the parents.

Full-moon Fridays bring angst to others outside of education, as well. Hospital ERs, ambulance personnel, crisis phone services, and police departments are all wary of full-moon Fridays, as accidents and injuries from bizarre events are more prevalent. Hospital, ambulance, and police administrators increase personnel and supplies during full-moon Fridays, as they know their staffs will be busier than any other day or night during the month.

Get ready for a wild ride, though, parents and school personnel at the middle school level!

Chapter 16

Athletes

Neil

I first met Neil when he was a 6th grade student. Stronger and taller than most of his peers, Neil excelled in football, basketball, and baseball throughout middle school.

He was also more aware of sexual language and practices, which he verbally displayed inappropriately all too frequently, on and off the fields of play and during bus trips to and from games. Numerous conversations, all to no avail, were held with Neil by coaches, his parents, with me, and others.

Neil went on to the local high school but never played sports, as he was charged and found guilty of sexual abuse early in his freshman year. Unfortunately, Neil has spent most of his adult years incarcerated for similar crimes. Seemingly, he, too, was another example of a student who never matured beyond the 7th grade level.

Baseball Team

Upon the realization that major league baseball was not in my future, I began to umpire baseball and softball games for the local city recreation department, while I completed my undergraduate classes. While these assignments could be from Little League to Open Division Fast-Pitch, each level of play had its own idiosyncratic and boisterous characters.

At the little league level, it was usually the parents in the stands. At the highest level of the fast-pitch softball leagues, it was usually the hyper shortstop that caused the most frustration. At the lower softball leagues it was, usually, the wives in the stands who were the most vocal and disruptive.

It was at the Pony League level of baseball, however, where most of the players were in the 7th grade, which provided the most disruptive behaviors.

One team's pitcher and catcher, in particular, exhibited this perfectly. While not happy with my umpiring behind the plate, the pitcher and catcher became more frustrated as the game went on. The catcher kept jerking pitches, which were obviously outside, to over the plate and the pitcher, "T.J.," complained often about my tight strike zone.

During the 5th inning of this particular game, I saw the catcher give a thumb's up signal in front of his chest protector. Since I knew of their frustration, I correctly assumed that this was a signal that I was to be hit by the next pitch. I gingerly encircled the straps on the back of the catcher's chest protector with my fingers and, as he started to slide out of the way during the pitch, I yanked him back into its path. The ball slammed off his own mask, much to his embarrassment and chagrin.

Their coach approached me, wondering what was going on. I explained to him what had happened and said it was actually pretty funny. Rightfully, though, he took both boys out of the game and sent them home with their parents.

Mario

While Mario never started for either of the two years I had him on one of my baseball teams, he was a positive influence on the others, working just as hard or harder than the others. He was rewarded with playing time towards the end of most games. His teammates rallied around him upon a successful hit or fielding accomplishment.

During one baseball tournament, in which we were playing for the championship trophy, Mario did not get into the game. He did coach down the first base line, however, whenever our team was at bat. He kept his mind in the game and offered insights, from his position by first, to his teammates.

Down by three runs in the last inning, I was looking for Mario to pinch hit. I left him alone, however, when I noticed him in the dugout on his knees, earnestly praying for us to win the game.

Mario and his wife recently celebrated their 25th anniversary and attend our bi-annual reunions. He remains actively and positively engaged with his extended family, with his church family, and in his community.

Darren

Darren was a 6th grader when I first met him. He, again, was the smallest boy in his class but was a pretty good athlete. Knowing his parents well, they invited me to attend one of his city-league basketball games.

Darren went to extreme lengths to gain acceptance from his peers and the spectators. He would occasionally drive the ball to the middle of the key, where the taller centers and forwards played. Unfortunately, he had no idea whatsoever of what to do with the ball when defended by those players and his attempted shots and passes were deflected often. Embarrassed upon being well guarded, Darren would feign an injury and be taken off the court, to the applause of the spectators. He would suddenly feel better about 5 minutes later and go back into the game, once again, with applause from the spectators.

As I was his basketball coach for his 7th grade year, I informed him and his father that I would not tolerate such behavior. As his coach, I explained to him that he must have a plan for the ball if he was going to drive the middle of the key. I further explained to he and his father, that I would have him dragged off the court, if he acted injured in any game I coached.

Our team went through about half the season before Darren did drive the middle with no plan. One of the players stuffed his shot and Darren went into his "act." He fell to the floor, holding his ankle and complaining loudly. As promised, I sent two players to drag him off the court.

Needless to say, he did not receive any applause from the crowd as they were, initially, stunned by my action. Luckily, Darren's father explained the full circumstances for my behavior to the crowd, and his wife, and the game continued without incident. Five minutes later, Darren announced that he was ready to get back into the game. I informed him that since he had "such a serious injury," I would be remiss in my duties to allow this; further eliminating another chance for applause from the crowd.

Darren never attempted to duplicate this behavior, in either the remaining of his 7th grade season nor during his 8th grade basketball season.

Darren went on to graduate from college and has had a successful career. His own sons are approaching this same grade level and I look forward to hearing from Darren's father how his grandsons perform.

"The" Football Team

Middle school students who play on city football teams or on cheerleading squads can be a royal pain in the butt! In more than one instance, team players and cheer squads were allowed to wear their game jerseys to school on Fridays, the day before their weekend games. Some used this "stature" to tease, taunt, and bully the other students who "didn't belong."

This is much more prevalent at the middle school level because the students don't, yet, fully understand the boundaries of what "team pride" should entail. Honestly, some of the coaches of these youth football teams were inadequately prepared, and sometimes just naïve, to fully and carefully explain this concept to their youthful teams.

As the negative behavior became evident at school, discussions were held about what actions we could take to stem the tide of such attitudes and behaviors. At every school where this was a problem, the logical answer was to no longer allow the uniforms to be worn.

Meetings with upset parents and coaches always ensued, with several teachers joining me in defining the behaviors and attitudes that were displayed on these "spirit" days. Without exception, the parents and coaches walked away with a fresh perspective and understood the rational for our decision.

While not every complaining staff member attended the sometimes heated and lively discussions with parents and coaches, I remain grateful for those who stepped up and assisted in defining the problem and supporting the decision.

In all cases, the parents and coaches of the athletes initially under the new guidelines explained to the upcoming athletes and their parents the reasons for them.

Chapter 17

Parents and Volunteers

Over the years, and at each school site, I have been blessed to experience a bevy of parents who volunteered. Some women volunteered in their child's classroom, acting as "room mothers," marking special occasions with special decorations or refreshments. This was, of course, before state regulations forbade homemade refreshments!

Parents of both sexes supported me when I sought School Board support and finances for new programs. Some attended field trips, drove to sports games when necessary, and some even attended Science Camp for an entire week! Others helped supervise during lunch recess or provided their knowledge by making presentations to a "Careers" or other exploratory class.

Upon my mother's death, one even organized with other parents and drove several of my students to attend the services in my support.

A truly "Unified" school district

While most school systems identify themselves as a "Unified School System," one southern Arizona district actually puts that concept into practice.

High School student "counselors" came to campus bi-weekly, as part of an elective class, to counsel elementary and middle school students and acting as "big brothers" or "big sisters" for those who felt invisible, unheard, or misunderstood.

Others took time out from their studies to act as chaperones at the annual 6th grade Science Camp for a week. In addition to their duties as cabin supervisors at night, they actively took an interest in the students under their supervision by encouraging the more nervous students to try, for example, picking up a horned toad, walking the "silent mile" alone and after dark, or kissing a banana slug!

As Principal, I drove over to Science Camp on Wednesdays of each week, to give those 6th graders that were feeling a little homesick, a quick glimpse of someone from "home" and to deliver letters from parents who had forgotten to mail their letters at the beginning of the week.

Such was the discipline from home and school that only one misbehaving attendee in all my years, as both teacher and administrator, did not successfully complete the week. Again, one of the many blessings I benefitted from in my 38 years.

The PTA

I was blessed to work alongside some great PTA leadership parents. They supported our school and teachers by recognizing special events with gifts or "goodies" in the teachers' lounge or in classrooms, by participating in sporting events or leagues that provided funds for extracurricular events, and through the purchasing of various classroom supplies.

As an incoming administrator, the PTA President often provided me an overview of the culture of the school and of the community. He or she would usually welcome parents to "Back to School Nights", to parent conferences, and to the graduation committee meetings. I viewed them as allies and revered them as supporters of our entire school community. To this day, I wish I had done more to recognize and thank them for their service and wisdom.

Above and Beyond

Two gentlemen were employed as correctional officers and counselors at the local county prison. They arrived in my office after initially seeing "gang colors" around our small, tight-knit community. Knowing that such activities usually begin at the middle school level, these two volunteered to meet with students who might be contemplating gang involvement.

They shared with these students the possible, and probable, outcomes of gang involvement. In addition to their own counseling, these two actually arranged for these students to visit the county prison to see prison life first-hand, to be locked up in a cell, and to be confronted by some of the prisoners about their behavior at school and in the community.

Was this "scared straight" approach successful? By all means! We saw the incidences of gang colors immediately and dramatically decrease and those who were involved in this counseling were in my office much less often.

A particular part of the program at the prison was most enlightening for the students, as related to me by several of them. During the tour of the facility, led by one of the correctional officers, the officer would point out a large orange placard above where the inmates congregated. He explained that if the correctional officer on duty had to fire his weapon, which occurred almost monthly, the first shot was to be into that placard.

"Do you see any sign whatsoever that the placard has received such a shot?" asked the guide. The placard was pristine and had never been damaged.

I remain ever grateful to these two volunteers, and impressed by their willingness to assist where they saw a need. They both moved up to do the same at the high school when they saw older students displaying gang colors or signs in the community. Additionally, one also volunteered as an Assistant Baseball Coach at the high school for a few years.

The two of them were so impressive that one parent shared with me that it was their positive example that provided the impetus for her to also seek a career in law enforcement!

Epilogue

It is my sincerest hope that the parent or educator reading this narrative has gleaned some insight into the mindset from which the immature boys' actions emanate. Please note that I didn't limit this last statement to the 7th grade because, as you now know, the questionable actions of the immature child and student actually start sooner than the 7th grade and, most often, last longer.

The underlying and unfulfilled need is one of acceptance, usually by his peers. This need might be shared, however, with circumstances that exist in the home: from cruelty by a sibling or parent; from a lack of parental participation in his life due to separation through divorce, death, or one's discomfort in showing affection; or, from the seemingly never-ending household moves which inhibit the formation of positive relationships with friends, classmates, and the educators in his everyday life. The probability, however, is that a combination of these circumstances has led to this delayed maturation process and the frustrating antics of the immature boy.

As a parent, single or in a committed relationship, I implore you to remain involved in this child's life. Do not allow your life circumstances to relegate his needs for a relationship, recognition, and acceptance to the back burner. He needs you to take an active role in his life to feel accepted, appreciated, understood, and loved.

Build upon this student's creative side, involving him in music, the performance arts, multimedia production, or fine art. Be quick to recognize even the initial small progress, as this will lead to feelings of acceptance and to greater progress thereafter. The more acceptance he feels in the home will decrease the need to seek acceptance, in negative ways, from his peers.

If building this positive relationship involves a coordinated effort with school or church personnel, take the time and steps necessary to build a team approach that will strengthen all his relationships and, thereby, reduce the need for disciplinary actions at home, at school, and in the community. If this involves a parent conference, do it. If this involves volunteering at school, do it.

As an educator, it is incumbent upon you to recognize this immaturity and the circumstances that initiate his actions. In order to do this, some form of investigation on your part is necessary, whether by conversing with parents and former teachers, by perusing his cumulative file kept in the office, or by talking with this student. Your proactive approaches will reduce the need for reactive disciplinary measures later.

As the more mature students in your class and school wait to see how the "new kid" behaves, purposefully team the immature student with a more mature and well-behaved student. Introductory practices like "mentor-for-a-day" programs, the use of "peer guides," and other team-building or introductory practices will enhance this "new beginning" for this student and give him an immediate sense of acceptance and, hopefully, quell his need to get acceptance in more disruptive manners.

Whether you are a classified employee, a teacher, counselor, or administrator, you can assist the immature student in many ways. Attendance and recognition for positive participation in sports, in the classroom, and out on the playground will have an immediate impact. School-wide programs, like the "All, for One." are powerful and will enhance positive student behaviors.

Being in front of the school upon the students' arrival, performing yard duty, visiting classes, counseling when needed, attending sporting events and dances, and offering accolades freely and often are meaningful actions an administrator can perform to, not only assist the immature student, but change the culture of the entire campus.

On a personal note, I neither condone nor encourage the use of corporal punishment in either the school or home. The negative effects are far greater in the long run than any temporary behavioral improvement.

Since alcohol use has been noted in this narrative, I do want the reader to know that my drinking has ceased. Given the choice of continued alcohol usage in social settings or the need for seizure medication to actually be effective, the choice to eliminate all alcohol was easy and has benefitted all my personal relationships.

Again, it is my deepest desire that both parents and educators can utilize my insights to have positive impacts in the lives of this "lower human life form" and assist them to realize their full potential as students, and eventual parents and community members.

Printed in the United States
By Bookmasters